Nothing to Read

Nothing to Read
Newspapers and Elections in a Social Experiment

Jeffery J. Mondak

Ann Arbor

THE UNIVERSITY OF MICHIGAN PRESS

Copyright © by the University of Michigan 1995
All rights reserved
Published in the United States of America by
The University of Michigan Press
Printed and bound by CPI Group (UK) Ltd, Croydon, CR0 4YY

2009   2008   2007   2006   5   4   3   2

A CIP catalog record for this book is available from the British Library.

Library of Congress Cataloging-in-Publication Data

Mondak, Jeffery J., 1962-
    Nothing to read : newspapers and elections in a social experiment
/ Jeffery J. Mondak.
       p.   cm.
    Includes bibliographical references and index.
    ISBN 978-0-472-09599-5 (alk. paper). — ISBN 978-0-472-06599-8 (pbk. :
alk. paper)
    1. Press and politics—United States.   2. Strikes and lockouts—
Newspapers—Pennsylvania—Pittsburgh.   3. Presidents—United
States—Elections—1992.   4. Congress—United States—
Elections, 1992.   I. Title.
PN4888.P6M66   1995
071'.3—dc20   95-16976
                                                            CIP

Chapter 4 is an adaptation of "Newspapers and Political Knowledge," *American
Journal of Political Science* 39, no. 2   (May 1995): 513–27. Reprinted with the
permission of The University of Wisconsin Press.

Chapter 5 is an adaptation of "Media Exposure and Political Discussion in U.S.
Elections," *Journal of Politics* 57, no. 1 (1995). By permission of the author and
the University of Texas Press.

ISBN 978-0-472-09599-5 (alk. paper)
ISBN 978-0-472-06599-8 (pbk. : alk. paper)

Acknowledgments

Numerous individuals and organizations have contributed greatly to this project. First, this study would not have been possible but for the 1992 Pittsburgh newspaper strike. Hence, the efforts, such as they were, of negotiators for the Pittsburgh Press Company and Teamsters' Local 211 are gratefully acknowledged. Second, on a more conventional note, this research was supported by a grant from the University of Pittsburgh's Central Research Development Fund, and by a research term provided by the Department of Political Science at the University of Pittsburgh. Data were collected by the University of Pittsburgh's Center for Social and Urban Research, under the supervision of Joyce Slater.

I worked with several research assistants in my first four years in Pittsburgh. The conscientious and responsible efforts of three graduate assistants have done much to improve my research. Kevin Olson served as a survey interviewer and also helped supervise data collection for this project. His contributions were instrumental in the timely and successful completion of data collection, and his efforts have greatly enriched this study. Damarys Canache and Mike Kulisheck worked primarily on other projects, freeing me to concentrate on the speedy completion of this book. An undergraduate assistant, Jeff Campbell, conducted an extensive content analysis that provided much of this study's supplementary data.

Many people offered helpful comments on the book manuscript, or on portions of the study that were delivered at academic conferences. I am thankful to Damarys Canache, Dave Heiss, Bob Huckfeldt, Jon Hurwitz, Diana Mutz, Vince Price, Tim Prinz, Bert Rockman, Alberta Sbragia, Shannon Smithey, Austin Works, Marilyn Yale, and Cliff Zukin. Thanks also to Malcolm Litchfield at the University of Michigan Press for both his encouragement and his assistance.

Chapter 4 is a modified version of a paper that appeared in the *American Journal of Political Science*, and chapter 5 is a revised version of a piece that was published in the *Journal of Politics*. I thank these journals and their editors for permission to use the material here.

Finally, I wish to thank the many candidates and their spokespersons who agreed to be interviewed for this project, and the 635 residents of the Cleveland and Pittsburgh metropolitan areas who graciously participated in this study's opinion survey.

Contents

Chapter

CHAPTER 1

Newspapers, Media, and Mass Politics

> If only for a minute or two
> I wanna see what it feels like to be without you
> —Lucinda Williams

Opportunity Knocked

Throughout the summer of 1992, I fretted about the future of an upcoming research project. The centerpiece of the study, which concerned contextual influence on electoral behavior, was to be a large postelection survey conducted in the Pittsburgh metropolitan area. With election day drawing nearer, the prospects for successful completion of the project appeared bleak. A strike had silenced the region's two major newspapers since mid-May, and an early settlement seemed unlikely. If the strike lasted through the entire election season, the generalizability of the study's results would be destroyed. After all, the absence of newspapers would fundamentally alter the information context, meaning that any insight the study produced regarding the dynamics of electoral behavior would be limited to those rather rare instances in which voters have no access to major local newspapers.

My first response to this situation was denial: the newspaper strike will be settled any day now, and the study will work out just fine. The second response, panic, set in by late July when it became clear that the Pittsburgh Press Company was not particularly interested in negotiating an end to the strike (newspapers ultimately did not return to Pittsburgh until mid-January, 1993). My third response to the strike was to view it as sheer good fortune. Rather than allowing social conditions to jeopardize the study of electoral behavior, I decided to design a new research project that would capitalize on those conditions. This book is the outcome. Methodologically, the research presented in this book hinges on one simple argument: one way to see if and how a thing is important to a society is to take that thing away, and then see what happens when it's gone.

This study's specific focus centers on the intersection of media and politics. Because Pittsburgh's newspaper strike encompassed the entire 1992 general election season, it creates a unique context in which to assess the significance of news media for electoral behavior. To gauge the importance of local newspapers to voters, we need only explore how voters reacted when those newspapers suddenly were no longer available. Building on this simple research strategy, this study capitalizes on the strike by using it as an opportunity to examine the particular electoral significance of local newspapers, along with media effects more generally. Further, because this study's unit of analysis is the voter, findings promise to shed new light on some of the fundamental questions central to the study of mass political behavior.

Opportunity alone does not provide sufficient grounds to justify a study's existence. Novelty is nice, but the study still must have something new to say. Because news media play the critical role of connecting citizens to politics, countless researchers have produced an enormous wealth of evidence regarding media's political significance. What new insight can be generated by a study centered on Pittsburgh's newspaper strike? The answer, I believe, is that this study can help to smooth what has been the most troubling stumbling point for investigators interested in the link between media and politics. Social science attempts to identify causal relationships among variables, and it attempts to represent the actual, or real-world, character of those connections. Meeting these objectives simultaneously always proves challenging, but the challenge seems particularly daunting when the research concerns the political significance of news media. Those studies that have been most successful in identifying causal relationships among variables have been conducted in the laboratory, producing ambiguity as to the real-world applicability of findings. Conversely, media research conducted in the field has identified numerous sets of correlates, but more often than not has failed to support conclusions regarding the direction of causality among those variables.

The unusual social conditions produced by Pittsburgh's newspaper strike created a singular opportunity to identify causal relationships while studying real-world media effects. This study's survey data were provided by actual voters who voted in actual elections. But the Pittsburgh voters also have much in common with participants in laboratory experiments, in the sense that their access to newspapers was abruptly denied—much the way subjects in laboratory studies face information contexts manipulated by the researcher. Further, data are drawn not just from Pittsburgh, but also from a demographically comparable area, Cleveland, where voters did have access to a major local newspaper in 1992. Comparison of electoral behavior in Cleveland and Pittsburgh will help to demonstrate the political significance of the local newspaper. Hence, at its core, this study's method is quasi-experimental. Internal and external validity are maximized within a single research design, linking the two threads that have threatened to unravel so many previous studies of the electoral significance of news media.

The purpose of this book is not merely to recount how voters reacted when their local newspapers were unavailable. Instead, voters' reactions will provide evidence regarding three aspects of electoral politics. The first and most direct question concerns the role of the local newspaper in U.S. elections. We can learn what unique effects newspapers play by measuring changes in mass behavior that occur in response to the sudden absence of those newspapers. Similarly, this study also may contribute to our general understanding of the electoral significance of news media. That is, in what ways might it matter to the voter if the media context is relatively information-poor? Finally, by studying how voters coped with the absence of newspapers, we may learn something about the voters themselves. For instance, do voters engage in an active information search prior to elections, or do they simply process the information that they encounter by chance during their everyday lives?

These questions will be addressed from several specific angles. The Pittsburgh and Cleveland survey data concern the 1992 presidential, Senate, and U.S. House elections. This multilevel focus allows attention to the possibility that the relationship between media and politics differs across electoral contexts. Four central empirical questions, the topics of chapters 3–6, will provide evidence regarding local newspapers, news media, and mass political behavior. First, patterns of information acquisition will be described. Where do people get their news about various elections, and what is the role of the local newspaper? The next issue is how much people learn from the news, and whether or not local newspapers are better suited than other media for conveying information about politics. The relationship between news media and social communication then will be examined to see if changes in the availability of news media alter interpersonal discussion about political campaigns. Finally, we will consider the link between information and the vote choice. In short, how do people use information when choosing among candidates, and what is the specific contribution of the local newspaper? Again, the methodological approach to these questions is quasi-experimental, because the empirical analyses center on the contrast between Cleveland and Pittsburgh, regions with and without access to a major local newspaper in 1992.

Detailed explanation of this study's quasi-experimental design appears in chapter 2. First, though, it is necessary to describe more fully the study's societal and scientific contexts. Hence, I turn now to a brief history of the Pittsburgh newspaper strike, and analysis of the strike's broad societal impact. Following that discussion, the central theoretical issues will be explored for each of this study's three broad themes: the electoral significance of the local newspaper; the more general political significance of news media; and the quality of mass political decision making. This chapter concludes with an overview of the material to be presented in subsequent chapters.

The 1992 Pittsburgh Newspaper Strike

On the evening of May 17, 1992, leaders of Teamsters' Local 211 stopped trucks from delivering the next morning's issues of the *Pittsburgh Post-Gazette*. What started as a Monday without newspapers eventually became an eight-month ordeal for the people of western Pennsylvania. The delivery trucks halted by the Teamsters were the property of the Pittsburgh Press Co. Because the *Press* and the *Post-Gazette* were run under a joint operating agreement, the strike silenced both of Pittsburgh's major daily newspapers.

For the Teamsters, the newspaper strike represented a struggle for survival, a fight against a proposal by the Pittsburgh Press Co. to cut 450 of 605 Teamster jobs. With literally nothing left to lose, the union's members saw no real reason not to wage a strike. It is perhaps this sense of desperation among the workers that partly accounted for the extraordinary length of time the city of Pittsburgh went without newspapers. In contrast with Pittsburgh's eight-month strike, for example, researchers previously have examined how the people of New York coped with strikes of less than three weeks in 1945 (Berelson [1949] 1979) and 1958 (Kimball 1959), and strikes of slightly more than three months in 1962 (Kimball 1963) and 1978 (Bogart 1989).

Early on, it was clear that negotiations between the Press Co. and the Teamsters were unproductive and increasingly hostile. Tension escalated considerably in late July, when the Press Co. tried for two days to publish their paper with the assistance of replacement workers. This attempt ended quickly in the face of strong opposition from the striking workers, many of the people of Pittsburgh, and numerous important community leaders. Thus, while the Democratic and Republican parties staged their national conventions, the citizens of western Pennsylvania endured a long summer without newspapers.

On October 2, 1992, E. W. Scripps Co., the parent of the Press Co., announced that the *Pittsburgh Press* was for sale. Corporate officials had decided that an amicable end to the strike was impossible, and that the *Press* would never again be a profitable player in the Scripps media empire. Ross Perot was back in the presidential race, the presidential debates were drawing near, and it was now certain that voters in the Pittsburgh area would not see the return of their newspapers prior to election day.

As the election came and went, the Pittsburgh Press Co. negotiated a sale with its rival, the *Post-Gazette*. Although the *Press* purportedly fielded at least two other offers, the former partners in a joint operating agreement soon finalized the sale. An end to the strike then was reached, but the cost for the people of Pittsburgh proved considerable: the 108-year-old *Pittsburgh Press*, the city's afternoon newspaper, and the stronger of Pittsburgh's two competing dailies, met its demise. The *Post-Gazette* resumed publication on a Monday morning exactly eight months after the start of the Teamsters' strike—January 18, 1993. But Pittsburgh was now a one-paper town.

Missing the Newspaper

The 1992 Pittsburgh newspaper strike was more than just an extended labor dispute. Instead, it was also a social phenomenon that altered the daily lives of hundreds of thousands of people. This book describes the political significance of missing the newspaper, drawing on the experiences of the people of Pittsburgh to gain new understanding of the relationship between news media and electoral politics. However, prior to analyzing the political consequences of the newspaper strike, it is useful to assess the broader social ramifications of the absence of newspapers. Electoral politics constitutes only a very small part of what goes on in a society. Thus, appreciation of the strike's more general effects provides context that will help later, when the focus centers specifically on the 1992 presidential, House, and U.S. Senate elections.

Prior to the strike, the daily circulation of the *Press* and the *Post-Gazette* totaled nearly 350,000. Hence, the sudden absence of the two daily newspapers created a substantial information vacuum. The first step in understanding the social consequences of the newspaper strike entails a summary of the major efforts by alternative media sources to fill this vacuum. Suburban newspapers and local broadcast media endeavored to fill the gap created when the *Press* and the *Post-Gazette* stopped publishing. However, the success of these media in compensating for the city's missing newspapers was rather limited.

Two suburban newspapers in the Pittsburgh area, the Greensburg *Tribune-Review* and the *North Hills News Record*, publish daily editions. The strike at the two major dailies created a window of opportunity for these smaller competitors, and both papers seized this chance to expand their circulations. Specifically, the *Tribune-Review* increased its daily circulation from 53,000 to 94,000, whereas the *North Hills News Record* nearly tripled its circulation, growing from 17,400 to 45,000. Although these gains were substantial, with nearly 70,000 additional issues of the suburban dailies being distributed, the growth in circulation reached only one-fifth of the *Press* and *Post-Gazette*'s collective prestrike daily circulation of 350,000. Thus, the suburban papers marginally reduced Pittsburgh's information vacuum, but a substantial gap remained.

Local television and radio also responded to the newspaper strike. However, although the length of daily news broadcasts was expanded, little additional substance emerged. With the same understaffed newsrooms struggling to fill a longer news slot, the end result rarely constituted a viable substitute for the daily newspapers. Three types of stories accounted for most of the added air time. First, there was more of the same. That is, the characteristic focus of local television on crime, fires, traffic, and the weather was simply broadened to include a few extra crimes, fires, and traffic jams each day. Second, the typical news broadcast was padded with the addition of one or two extra wire-service stories. Third, in a curious effort to replicate some of the more unique functions of the local newspaper, the television stations scrolled seemingly endless strings of classified ads and obituaries.

Nationally, to minimize operating expenses local broadcast media typically rely on very cost-efficient sources such as releases from local public relations offices (Graber 1993). One important source is the local newspaper (McManus 1990); the newspaper sets the local news agenda, and broadcast media follow the paper's lead. McManus (1990) found evidence of this type of relationship not only in small media markets, but also in markets comparable to Pittsburgh in size. Given such reliance on newspapers, local broadcast media are not well suited to step in when those newspapers become unavailable. Hence, the failure of Pittsburgh's television and radio stations to add more substantive reporting to their expanded news broadcasts perhaps should not be considered surprising. Nevertheless, one clear point remains: the information gap created by the newspaper strike remained sizable despite compensatory efforts by alternative media sources.[1]

Previous studies examining how former readers coped with newspaper strikes reported that many individuals expressed a strong sense of loss when their papers were unavailable (Kimball 1959, 1963; Bogart 1989). Similar feelings seemed prevalent during Pittsburgh's lengthy strike. Among its many functions, the local newspaper provides an important focal point for a community. Many simple examples demonstrate the broad reach of the newspaper. For instance, without a newspaper, how does a family advertise its garage sale or learn what movies are playing at the local theater? The effort by Pittsburgh's local television stations to report obituaries morbidly exemplifies one of the unique roles of the local newspaper.

Additional evidence that the people of Pittsburgh missed their striking newspapers comes from the world of professional sports. Pittsburgh's three major sports teams—the Penguins of the National Hockey League, baseball's Pirates, and football's Steelers—all reached the play-offs during the course of the strike. However, without newspapers, public response was somewhat muted. Attendance at Pirates' games declined substantially from the previous season, a fact team officials attributed partly to the absence of newspapers. For many fans, baseball is less engaging if they cannot peruse the daily standings and box scores. Likewise, when the Penguins won hockey's Stanley Cup, there was no banner headline to proclaim the victory. I lived in Detroit when the Tigers won baseball's World Series in 1984, and the next day's newspapers helped to crystallize the city's feeling of celebration. That feeling was missing in Pittsburgh in 1992.

For most people, newspapers are simply a part of everyday life. Some people read the paper to keep informed, others to relax, and some just to have something to do. During Pittsburgh's newspaper strike, many family members probably saw each others' faces at breakfast for the first time in years. Other people switched brands of cereal and toothpaste just to get something new to read. My basset hound puppy was conference-paper-trained. The local newspaper plays a central role in its community, and that influence may well extend to the arena of electoral politics. Thus, a strike that was misfortune for the people of Pittsburgh provides a unique opportunity for social science—the opportunity to acquire new insight about the relationship between news media and electoral behavior.

Local Newspapers, News Media, and Mass Political Behavior

By abruptly altering the region's information context, the strike can help to provide new perspective on the electoral significance of the local newspaper. Moving beyond this relatively specific issue, we also will consider media effects more broadly, and explore the meaning of empirical findings for the quality of mass political decision making. These three areas of inquiry—local newspapers, media effects, and mass political behavior—have been the subjects of a great many empirical studies and theoretical discussions. Therefore, a brief review of the questions central to each area is needed to help form a framework from which to examine what happened in Pittsburgh and Cleveland in 1992.

Local Newspapers

Newspapers quite obviously make available a great quantity of information. Further, it is clear that by virtue of their format local newspapers possess certain advantages over alternative information sources such as television. However, the simple fact that newspapers differ in format from competing news sources does not ensure that readers receive news or interpretations from newspapers that could not be acquired elsewhere. Some people prefer to get their news from television, some from radio or news magazines, and some from newspapers. In studying the societal and political implications of the local newspaper, we must ask if the individual's selection of a primary news source affects that person's subsequent political knowledge and behavior. In other words, does the local newspaper offer a *unique* contribution to the information base of the American public?

In recent years, researchers rarely have focused their attention specifically on the local newspaper. Instead, television news has received the greatest scrutiny in media studies, particularly in those studies concerning media and electoral behavior. However, many analysts have examined the political significance of television news by contrasting television with newspapers. Hence, comparisons concerning format, story content, and audience response provide evidence relevant to the question of whether or not the local newspaper offers some unique contribution. Additionally, several investigations regarding media coverage of U.S. House campaigns have used local newspapers as the primary source for data concerning the content of media reports.

The conventional thinking holds that newspapers outperform broadcast media in conveying information to their audiences (e.g., Davis 1992; Graber 1993). More specifically, newspapers purportedly excel in transmitting detailed factual data, an advantage that enables the papers' readers to learn more about current affairs than persons exposed only to broadcast media (e.g., Robinson and Levy 1986; Robinson and Davis 1990; Berkowitz and Pritchard 1989; Weaver and Drew 1993). Simply put, it is hypothesized that people who read the newspaper will generally learn more than people who watch television.

This theory of print superiority enjoys a strong degree of intuitive appeal. Compared to television news, the format of newspapers clearly appears to be more conducive to information acquisition. First, a newspaper contains much more information than does the typical television news broadcast. If more information is available, it is certainly plausible that more information actually will be received by the consumer. Second, television's emphasis on visual imagery possibly detracts from attention to factual data, contextual details, and analysis of abstract concepts. In contrast, newspaper reports are able to focus on a story's more difficult subtle nuances. Third, exposure to a newspaper is self-paced. That is, readers can take as much or as little time to peruse any particular story as they see fit. Television news broadcasts neither pause to let the viewer ponder the implications of a story, nor let the viewer skip past uninteresting reports.

Evidence in support of the notion of print superiority comes mostly from survey research. Typically, analysts gather data on respondents' patterns of media exposure and on their knowledge of current affairs. Statistical treatments of these data reveal that individuals whose primary news source is the newspaper tend to have higher knowledge levels than persons who acquire news mainly from broadcast media (e.g., Robinson and Levy 1986; Gunter 1987). In their most sophisticated form, studies of this type demonstrate that the relationship between exposure to print media and information acquisition withstands the introduction of controls for individual-level factors such as education. Further, the apparent general capacity of newspapers to foster learning may extend to the more specific realm of electoral politics. For example, two extensive studies (Patterson and McClure 1976; Patterson 1980) have produced sharp criticism of television's coverage of elections, providing domain-specific corroboration of the relative superiority of print media.

Taken at face value, the finding that people learn more from newspapers than from broadcast media clearly supports the premise that newspapers offer a unique contribution to the information base of the American public. However, several critics have recently warned that past research possibly creates the appearance of print superiority when no such superiority may, in reality, exist (e.g., Graber 1990; Price and Zaller 1993; Neuman, Just, and Crigler 1992). People whose primary news source is the newspaper tend to have relatively high levels of education, prior political knowledge, interest in current affairs, cognitive skill, and so on. It may be these factors, rather than exposure to newspapers, that explain why newspaper readers understand current affairs better than their television-viewing counterparts. In other words, newspaper readers are a self-selected lot, and the individual-level traits they share may drive information acquisition. If this is the case, then evidence of print superiority merely would signify a spurious relationship.

Price and Zaller (1993) use survey data to examine the relationship between media exposure and information acquisition. However, rather than relying on coarse indicators of attentiveness such as education, Price and Zaller introduce a measure of prior political knowledge. When this variable is included in statistical models, newspaper exposure generally proves to be unrelated to news recall. Neuman, Just, and Crigler (1992) report similar results with data drawn from laboratory experiments. The authors find no consistent relationship between news medium and political knowledge when controls are introduced to account for the cognitive skill of the study's participants. Further, in contrast with the conventional wisdom, Neuman, Just, and Crigler demonstrate that in some contexts broadcast media may outperform newspapers in fostering information acquisition.

Proponents of print superiority may question the critical control variables introduced in the Price and Zaller (1993) and Neuman, Just, and Crigler (1992) studies. For example, it may be the case that a lifetime of exposure to newspapers contributes to a person's prior political knowledge as measured by Price and Zaller. Likewise, reading the newspaper may hone the cognitive skills discussed by Neuman, Just, and Crigler. Additionally, the laboratory context of the Neuman, Just, and Crigler study possibly intensified participants' levels of attention to the project's television news stories, overcoming the important real-world differences in format that distinguish newspapers from television. In the laboratory, there are no ringing telephones, barking dogs, or crying babies to distract the television viewer's attention.

Although evidence abounds on both sides, it is clear that doubt remains regarding the relative capacity of newspapers to facilitate information acquisition. Fortunately, the Pittsburgh newspaper strike provides a distinctive new avenue from which to approach this question. If newspapers offer a unique contribution to information levels in a society, then the sudden and prolonged absence of those newspapers should produce a detectable drop in knowledge of current affairs. Hence, the strike functions much like an experimental manipulation, but one that is imposed upon an entire metropolitan area rather than just a small group of laboratory subjects. Because *everybody* in the region was denied access to a major local newspaper, the strike enables us to cut through the tangled web of causality faced in many previous studies. If the capacity of newspapers to foster political learning is unmatched by other media, then we should find evidence that knowledge levels among the people of Pittsburgh declined due to the city's eight-month newspaper strike.

Although most previous studies of newspaper effects have considered the general advantages of newspapers relative to broadcast media, it is possible that the impact of newspapers is context-specific. This point rings particularly true in the arena of electoral politics. For example, the newspaper versus television comparison will potentially produce very different results when we move from the presidential race to Senate elections, and from Senate elections to U.S. House contests. For House races, for example, local newspapers may dominate media coverage due to the poor fit between House districts and most media markets (Clarke and Evans 1983; Campbell, Alford, and Henry 1984; Simmons 1987; Vermeer 1987a). In the Pittsburgh area, four U.S. House districts contain cities in Allegheny County, and two additional districts include other areas within easy reach of Pittsburgh's broadcast media. In contexts such as this, it is simply bad business for a television news report to devote meaningful attention to any single House race because the vast majority of viewers will not be residents of the district in question. Where television coverage of House races is minimal, voters may turn to newspapers by default. Thus, whatever their more general effects, newspapers may offer a unique contribution to citizens' understanding of certain aspects of current affairs for the simple reason that alternative media coverage is just not available.

This study includes data concerning the presidential, Senate, and U.S. House elections.[2] Consequently, a comparative focus can be invoked, enabling simultaneous examination of newspaper effects in presidential and subpresidential campaigns (see also Clausen et al. 1992). Thus, the fundamental issue of whether or not local newspapers uniquely contribute to the information base of the American electorate will be reexamined both on a general level and within the context of three specific types of political campaigns.

Media Effects

The possibility that local newspapers offer a singular contribution in U.S. elections presupposes that media matter. If the information that media convey to voters has no impact on the dynamics of electoral behavior, then local newspapers, as a subset of the media industry, also must bring no influence. Therefore, study of the broad question of media effects provides essential context for assessment of the specific influence associated with the local newspaper.

Intuitively, the question of media effects leads one to answer that yes, of course media matter in U.S. elections. Nearly everything that voters know about candidates presumably originates with news coverage. Media connect people with politics, exposing voters to information and events that they simply could not experience directly. Therefore, media surely must hold considerable influence on the course of electoral behavior. Curiously, however, the empirical evidence has not kept pace with intuition. Bartels (1993, 267) makes the point well:

> The state of research on media effects is one of the most notable embarrassments of modern social science. The pervasiveness of the mass media and their virtual monopoly over the presentation of many kinds of information must suggest to reasonable observers that what these media say and how they say it has enormous social and political consequences. Nevertheless, the scholarly literature has been much better at refuting, qualifying, and circumscribing the thesis of media impact than at supporting it.

The notion that news media make little difference in political campaigns originated with Lazarsfeld, Berelson, and Gaudet's (1944) study of voting in the 1940 election (see also Katz 1957; Klapper 1960). The Columbia authors' minimal-effects view hinges on two central points. First, media's campaign coverage purportedly does not shape or change voting preferences, but instead merely reinforces predispositions that existed prior to the onset of the campaign. Second, any potential for direct influence associated with news media is constrained by the existence of a two-step flow of information. From this perspective, only a small core of opinion leaders actively attend to the news. These individuals filter and interpret the news before conveying it to the mass public through social communication.

Researchers attempting to counter the minimal effects thesis have been plagued by difficulty in measuring media effects. If media coverage is always present, and if exposure to that coverage is widespread, then we are left with an explanatory factor that does not vary. A further complication is the questionable utility of survey respondents' self-reports of media exposure. It is simply unreasonable to expect respondents to recall precisely how many hours of television news they have viewed, or where they first learned about a particular news event. Survey respondents may provide answers based on projections or stereotypes rather than accurate recall, a point demonstrated well in Lodge, McGraw, and Stroh's (1989) discussion of responses to the candidate-evaluation items included on many postelection surveys. Consequently, media effects may exist, yet elude the grasp of social science.

Bartels (1993) offers a statistical refinement to address both the problem of measurement error in survey data and the limitations of cross-sectional research designs.[3] His findings strongly challenge the minimal-effects thesis. First, Bartels demonstrates that the impact of media exposure on opinion change during the 1980 presidential campaign appears much greater once corrections are introduced to account for measurement error. Second, Bartels argues that exclusive focus on short-term and direct effects understates media's true influence. From this perspective, the availability of data that better capture media's possible indirect and long-term effects likely would provide further evidence that media do matter.

Laboratory experiments offer a second means of reconsidering the question of media influence. The most prominent work in this tradition is that of Iyengar and Kinder (1987; Iyengar 1991). Iyengar and Kinder's study of television news indicates that news media hold considerable sway in two areas. First, the agenda-setting effect occurs when "those problems that receive prominent attention on the national news become the problems the viewing public regards as the nation's most important" (Iyengar and Kinder 1987, 16). Second, the priming effect occurs when media pay disproportionate attention to some issues and events rather than others, because by doing so "television news influences the standards by which governments, presidents, policies, and candidates for public office are judged" (Iyengar and Kinder 1987, 63). The authors' experiments yield compelling support for the agenda-setting and priming hypotheses, suggesting that the political significance of media is considerable. However, it is noteworthy that agenda setting and priming are more subtle forces than the direct effects sought by media researchers a generation earlier.

The Bartels (1993) and Iyengar and Kinder (1987) studies are among the most recent and the most methodologically sophisticated responses to the minimal-effects thesis of the 1940s. Cumulatively, such evidence on media effects clearly supports the premise that media do matter. Nevertheless, this is not an entirely comfortable conclusion. Many recent studies have chipped away at the minimal-effects perspective, yet the extent to which media coverage ultimately affects electoral choice remains unclear. It is particularly disconcerting that the strongest evidence of media effects emerges only when researchers either enter the pristine confines of the laboratory or rely on specialized data sets and statistical methods. If media are truly influential, evidence of that influence perhaps should not be so elusive.

Fortunately, the research opportunity created by Pittsburgh's newspaper strike allows new leverage on the question of media effects in U.S. elections. Although the strike certainly is no methodological panacea, it will be revealing to examine how voting behavior did or did not change when voters' access to news media was suddenly constrained.[4] Pittsburgh voters were without their local newspapers for the final presidential primaries, the Democratic and Republican conventions, and the entire general election season. If media matter, then this extended information drought should produce detectable influence on the voting behavior of Pittsburgh residents.

In considering whether media matter in U.S. elections, a significant question is often overlooked: compared to what? If the information that drives electoral choice does not originate with news media, then what is the source of that information? Although the likely alternatives seem few in number, one viable possibility is the voter's social networks. People talk about politics and elections, and the substance of that interpersonal discussion influences the vote (Huckfeldt and Sprague 1995). However, the existence of socially transmitted information brings no obvious implications for the electoral role of news media. It may be that media and discussion compete as information sources; some voters rely primarily on media for their campaign news while others rely on interpersonal discussion. Indeed, such a perspective comports well with the idea of a two-step information flow. However, if the information transmitted through social networks originates with news media,[5] then it might be best to view media and discussion as complementary information sources rather than as competitors.

One objective of this study is to address whether news media and political discussion are competitors or complements. Evidence relevant to the question of information exposure will emerge if Pittsburgh's newspaper strike prompted an increase or decrease in the frequency with which voters engaged in interpersonal political discussion. If voters treat political discussion and news media as alternative information sources, then we should see a boost in the quantity of political discourse by voters attempting to devise substitutes for their missing newspapers. Conversely, if news media provide the topics for political discussion, then the strike may have diminished voters' propensity to talk about the 1992 campaigns. Further, given that political discussion previously has been found to affect the vote choice, the strike provides an opportunity to determine if media exposure moderates that effect. That is, does the influence of political discussion on the direction of electoral choice vary as a function of the voter's access to the campaign coverage provided by news media? It is possible, for instance, that discussion is most significant as a determinant of electoral choice when the voter is not able to come to a decision on the basis of information available elsewhere.

In addition to the campaign-specific information conveyed by news media and social communication, voters may also draw on more stable or long-term information when deciding which candidates to support. For example, it is well established that partisanship and incumbency are critical factors in many campaigns, and particularly in congressional elections (e.g., Flanigan and Zingale 1991; Jacobson 1992). Does the strength of such forces serve to demonstrate the minimal-effects thesis, or does the information reported by news media limit voters' reliance on these simple cues? Once again, assessment of how Pittsburgh voters reacted to the absence of their newspapers will be revealing. For example, evidence that Pittsburgh voters were unusually reliant on partisan or incumbency cues in 1992 would suggest that such cues function as default mechanisms, establishing by implication the significance of campaign-specific information conveyed by news media.

We know, of course, that local newspapers and other news media do provide extensive coverage of national political campaigns. News gets reported. Hence, the search for media effects and for evidence of the specific influence of newspapers ultimately constitutes a means to evaluate the process of information acquisition. We want to know what voters do with the information news media convey, and what this means for electoral politics. In short, what does the nature of information acquisition imply regarding the quality of American electoral behavior?

Electoral Behavior

This book examines media effects with particular focus on the relationship between news media and electoral choice. Media quite obviously will matter in elections only if information is important to voters. If the vote choice is constructed on the basis of stable preferences, with little or no attention by voters to information specific to the individual political campaign, then the possible consequences of news media in U.S. elections will be few. Conversely, if voters systematically seek relevant information prior to deciding which candidates to support, then the availability and content of media coverage may be highly influential. Thus, how we characterize the American voter creates a framework for the study of media effects. Unfortunately, the task of assessing the deliberative skill of the American electorate brings both complexity and controversy.

Effective democratic governance requires a citizenry capable of meaningful political participation. However, the extent to which this standard is met in the United States has been strongly questioned. Indeed, evaluation of the political aptitude of the American voter constitutes the central area of debate among students of mass political behavior in the United States. Some factors are not in dispute. For example, most analysts accept that voters' levels of textbook civics knowledge tend to be quite low, and that only a small portion of the electorate possesses a view of politics structured on a meaningful sense of ideology.

But what such evidence means for democratic governance remains in doubt. We simply have no fixed set of criteria by which to judge whether public input to the political system retains sufficient substantive content for representation to flourish.

Normative theories and early economic models of electoral choice both depict the voter as a conscientious, well-informed, and deliberative decision maker. Unfortunately, several decades of empirical research have produced evidence in stark contrast with this ideal, painting instead a rather gloomy picture of the American electorate. By now, the tale is quite familiar. The Columbia studies, conducted in the 1940s, found most voters to lack much interest in politics or knowledge of the candidates. Electoral choice was not driven by cautious assessment of the candidates and their positions, but instead represented the predictable consequence of stable social characteristics (Lazarsfeld, Berelson, and Gaudet 1944; Berelson, Lazarsfeld, and McPhee 1954). Soon after, of course, the Michigan researchers (Campbell et al. 1960) reported further evidence regarding the lack of sophistication of the typical American voter. The authors identified an electorate essentially incapable of comprehending debates over contemporary political issues. Lacking an issue focus, Campbell and his colleagues claimed that electoral choice was determined largely by stable partisan preferences.

A considerable body of subsequent evidence supported this sharply pessimistic view. Converse (1964) offered a highly influential critique of the American electorate, demonstrating that for most voters, understanding of politics was hampered by a virtual absence of ideological structure. Likewise, a vast number of researchers have shown Americans to hold disturbingly low levels of knowledge about both the workings of their government and the central points of major policy disputes (see Kinder 1983; Kinder and Sears 1985; Neuman 1986). It appears that voters do not know very much, that what knowledge they do possess is not organized particularly well, and that few voters show any interest in evaluating the issues debated within electoral campaigns. This worst-case scenario suggests that democratic governance in the United States is essentially vacuous. From this perspective, news media enjoy no real opportunity to offer a meaningful contribution to the electoral system; where the audience is unconcerned, the messenger will be inconsequential.

This critical depiction of the American electorate has not gained universal acceptance. Indeed, numerous rebuttals began to appear soon after publication of *The American Voter* (Campbell et al. 1960) and Converse's (1964) analysis of belief systems. In the past 10 years, for example, an emerging research tradition has cast the American voter in a relatively favorable light, suggesting that warnings of the demise of democratic representation in the United States may be nothing more than false alarms. Research in the field of "political cognition"[6] draws on social psychological theories of information processing and decision making in reexamining the fundamental dynamics of mass political behavior (e.g., Lau and Sears 1986; Ferejohn and Kuklinski 1990; Sniderman, Brody, and Tetlock 1991; Page and Shapiro 1992; Iyengar and McGuire 1993; Iyengar and Ottati 1994). In social psychology, theorists commonly argue that humans partly overcome our inherent limitations as information processors. Simon's (1957) description of "bounded rationality," Fiske and Taylor's (1991) notion of humans as "cognitive misers," and Chaiken's (Chaiken, Liberman, and Eagly 1989) "sufficiency principle" all suggest that people can offer judgments with meaningful structure even in the absence of extensive deliberation. Research in political cognition builds on this basic premise, establishing that voters need not fully comprehend the intricacies and technical points of politics and government for democratic representation to flourish.

Broadly, the cognitive perspective holds that voters draw on a variety of efficiency mechanisms that help to simplify political decision making. With the aid of decision cues, simple rules of judgment, schematic structures, and so on, the individual can construct a meaningful judgment without scrutinizing all available information. It may be correct that voters possess neither tightly constrained belief systems nor much factual knowledge about politics, but those truths are insufficient to establish that political judgments are random or unstructured. Simply put, a low level of political knowledge does not preclude the individual from functioning as a capable political participant.

Popkin's (1991) defense of "the reasoning voter" exemplifies the new understanding that can be gained by applying social psychologists' conceptions of information processing to the study of electoral behavior. According to Popkin, voters are driven by "low-information rationality." Armed with various bits and scraps of relevant information, people use simple but reliable decision rules to construct their assessments of political candidates. The voter may not engage in an exhaustive critique of the candidates, but the voter does process available information prior to deciding which candidates to support. Hence, the relevance and accessibility of information are central to our understanding of the reasoning voter's political preferences. From this perspective, news media potentially play a highly important role in electoral politics because the focus of news coverage largely determines what information the voter is likely to receive.

Although political cognition provides grounds for optimism, most research in this tradition merely establishes that the quality of mass political decision making exceeds purely random or arbitrary action. Considerable territory exists on the continuum between random and fully informed decision making, but research in political cognition has not yet pinpointed where on that continuum we should place the typical voter's evaluative process. Data regarding the reaction of voters to Pittsburgh's newspaper strike will help considerably in the effort to assess just how rational low-information rationality actually is. Hence, although this study's results will directly concern the influence of newspapers and media, the implications of those results for the quality of electoral behavior also will be discussed.

Consider three examples of the types of questions that this study may help to address. First, data will reveal the extent to which voters tailor the information search on an election-specific basis. If voters are content to process only that information which is most available, regardless of its applicability for a particular political race, then we should expect the quality of electoral choice to vary for different elections. For instance, casual exposure to national broadcast media may provide the voter with a great abundance of information relevant to the presidential election, but very little information pertinent to the House vote. Thus, if the voter follows a single information-acquisition strategy for all elections, the information base will be more appropriate for some contests than for others. In this case, the vote choice would be something more than random, yet we would still be reluctant to praise such a unidimensional decision-making strategy. In contrast, evidence that voters conduct a unique information search for each election would indicate the existence of an active and adaptive electorate, one that balances the desire for efficiency in decision making with the reality of an inconsistent and limited information base.

Second, the newspaper strike provides a context in which we can assess the strength of the voter's motivation to construct reliable evaluations of candidates. When the going gets tough—such as when an entire region suddenly is denied access to local newspapers—does the voter invest the time and effort needed to modify the information search, or does the individual simply base the vote choice on a more limited information set? If, for example, local newspapers previously constituted a voter's primary source of news about political campaigns, studying how this individual reacts to the absence of newspapers will be revealing. The conscientious or motivated voter would augment the information search in an attempt to compensate for the absence of newspapers, whereas the relatively unconcerned voter would simply fall back on existing secondary information sources.

A third question arises if Pittsburgh voters drew on the assistance of simple decision cues to help overcome the absence of their newspapers. That is, how useful are those cues? Popkin (1991) argues, for example, that partisanship provides a default judgment when reliable campaign-specific information is not available. If Pittsburgh voters turned to partisanship or to other similar cues, we can assess the level of structure characteristic of the resulting vote choices.

By framing such questions within the context of political cognition research, study of the electoral significance of the newspaper strike promises to contribute new perspective on the rationality and skill of the American voter. This objective provides a focal point for the coming chapters, together with the goal of obtaining evidence pertaining to the more specific questions of newspaper and media effects.

Plan of the Book

This study's quasi-experimental design is described in chapter 2. Methodologically, my goal in this book is to identify causal relationships while examining real-world media effects. In chapter 2, review of the strengths and weaknesses of survey research and of laboratory experiments reveals the complementary nature of these methods—laboratory methods allow us to pinpoint causal relationships, whereas survey data help us to understand actual social phenomena as they exist outside of the laboratory. Therefore, my two-part methodological objective requires combination of the relative strengths of laboratory experiments and survey research within a single methodological framework. Toward this end, chapter 2 details the survey that provides the bulk of this study's data, and explains the quasi-experimental structure that will underlie analysis of those data.

Chapter 3 examines patterns of media exposure. In one sense, this chapter constitutes an extended manipulation check because it focuses on how Pittsburgh's newspaper strike affected the media-use patterns of the region's residents. Specifying those effects is a necessary prerequisite for the analyses to be conducted in the following three chapters. However, the question of media exposure is also important in itself. In chapter 3, we will consider where voters received their news about the 1992 presidential, Senate, and House campaigns, and whether voters tailored the information search on an election-specific basis. Further, analysis of how Pittsburgh residents adapted to the absence of newspapers will provide preliminary evidence regarding both the electoral significance of local newspapers and the flexibility of the American voter.

Chapter 4 is the first segment in a three-part examination of specific media effects. Political knowledge is the focus of chapter 4. Returning to the debate concerning the possibility that newspapers outperform other media in fostering political learning, this chapter presents data regarding the effect of the strike on voters' knowledge levels. We see if the absence of newspapers limited actual knowledge levels in three general domains: noncampaign current affairs; the horse-race aspect of the 1992 elections; and the presidential candidates' policy positions. Additional evidence indicates respondents' perceptions of the impact of newspapers on their knowledge about the presidential, Senate, and House campaigns.

News media are not an individual's only source of information about politics and elections. As we have seen, one important alternative is interpersonal political discussion. Chapter 5 explores the relationship between media and discussion, with particular emphasis on the question of whether this relationship is conflicting or complementary. The first issue is information exposure. That is, does the voter choose between news media and political discussion as information sources, or does exposure to one heighten attentiveness to the other? The second issue is influence. For example, does the guiding force of political discussion on an individual's vote choice vary in magnitude as a function of how much information the individual has received from news media? Once again, the newspaper strike provides a simple means to examine these questions, because we need only see how the dynamics of interpersonal discussion were changed by the strike to gain purchase on the relationship between news media and discussion.

In electoral politics, the bottom line is the vote. Simply put, we want to know what factors help to explain why the voter supported one candidate rather than another. The importance of news media for the vote is examined in chapter 6. Drawing on psychological theories regarding the efficiency mechanisms prevalent in human decision making, chapter 6 considers whether the pervasiveness of reliance on simple voting cues varies in response to the voter's access to information from news media. For example, is partisan-based voting a default mechanism for individuals who lack the information base to construct election-specific judgments? Also, do media effects vary depending on the strength of the voter's partisan attachment? Questions such as these are considered in chapter 6 with data regarding the vote choice in the 1992 presidential, Senate, and House elections.

The data and analysis presented in chapters 2–6 provide evidence relevant to this study's three fundamental questions: the political significance of local newspapers, the general role of news media in elections, and the aptitude of the American voter. Chapter 7 returns to these three issues, integrating the previous chapters' empirical findings. As we will see, results often conflict with the conventional wisdom, suggesting many interesting implications concerning the role of news media in U.S. elections. Therefore, chapter 7 concludes with recommendations for changes in media practices that would potentially improve the process of information acquisition for the American voter.

CHAPTER 2

A Methodological Overview

Sometimes you're the windshield
Sometimes you're the bug
— Mark Knopfler

The 1992 Pittsburgh newspaper strike provides the basis for a social experiment. By studying how voters responded when newspapers were unavailable, new understanding can be gained regarding the electoral significance of the local newspaper. However, for such insight to emerge, it is necessary to move from a broad focus on the strike to the design of a specific methodological strategy that capitalizes on these unique social conditions. This study's method is quasi-experimental, combining elements of the opinion survey and the laboratory experiment. Like all research methods in the social sciences, the approach taken here has both strengths and weaknesses. Because it is important to understand these strengths and weaknesses, the study's quasi-experimental design is examined in detail in this chapter.

Laboratory experiments and public-opinion surveys have generated great bodies of invaluable data regarding media and politics. However, both of these methods also suffer significant methodological limitations. Thus, because this study draws on both experimental and survey techniques, review of the fundamental elements of experimental and survey research provides context and foundation for assessment of this study's quasi-experimental design. The starting point is a brief discussion of the respective methodological advantages and disadvantages of the survey and the experiment. Following that discussion, I will describe how elements of experimental and survey research have been merged to create this study's unique quasi-experimental framework.

Researching Media Effects

Numerous methodological strategies have been employed by analysts concerned with the impact of news media on mass political behavior. The two most common approaches for examining media effects both involve attention to the actions of individual citizens. One approach centers on the study of survey data. Drawing on data from opinion surveys, the researcher attempts to identify dimensions of political behavior that are correlated with particular media-use patterns. For example, the researcher might measure voters' knowledge of political affairs and their exposure to different media sources in an effort to determine whether broadcast or print media best promote information acquisition. A second methodological approach in investigating media effects is for the researcher to conduct scientific experiments. In the laboratory experiment, the investigator again hopes to learn about some aspect of the relationship between media and individual-level political behavior. The distinguishing feature of laboratory research is the capacity to manipulate key variables. For example, the question of information acquisition might be examined by exposing one group of participants to print media, exposing a second group to broadcast media, and then comparing the groups' resulting knowledge levels.

The survey and the experiment are best viewed as complements. One method's strong suit is the other's Achilles heel. At bottom, survey research typically is strong at external validity, whereas experimental research is strong at internal validity. Of course, internal validity and external validity both are essential if a study's results are to generate meaningful new insight about a social or political phenomenon. By understanding what it is that provides the survey and the experiment with their respective strengths, we can determine how internal and external validity may be simultaneously maximized within a single quasi-experimental research design.

Survey Research

The primary strength of scientific opinion research is generalizability, or external validity. When respondents are drawn randomly from a population, the opinions of a relatively small number of individuals will represent the opinions of the general population with a high level of accuracy.[1] Due largely to this critical methodological strength, survey research has produced considerable advancements in our understanding of a diverse array of social and political phenomena.

Social scientists usually are interested in identifying causal relationships. We want to know what causes what. Unfortunately, data from opinion surveys rarely contribute conclusive evidence regarding the direction of causality. In short, internal validity is lacking (for a valuable discussion of this point, see Iyengar and Kinder 1987, chap. 2). The survey may produce evidence that two variables are correlated. However, the analyst typically will be able to offer only conjecture on the question of why those two variables covary. Arguably, this limitation of survey research is the leading source of overstated conclusions in the social sciences. Simply placing a variable on the right side of a regression equation does not establish that that factor is cause rather than effect.

Suppose, for example, that survey research produces evidence that those individuals with the highest levels of exposure to media coverage of a political campaign also report the highest levels of interpersonal discussion about that campaign. Again, the analyst wants to know what causes what. In this instance, there are at least four plausible explanations for the identified correlation. First, media exposure may fuel political discussion. Individuals with the highest levels of exposure to campaign news simply have more to talk about. Second, interpersonal discussion may heighten attentiveness to news reports. If discussion piques a voter's interest, then increased levels of media exposure will follow. Third, media exposure and political discussion may exert simultaneous influence on one another. Media provide topics for discussion, and discussion motivates further media exposure. Finally, media exposure and political discussion may be correlated because a third factor influences them both. For example, interest in politics may affect levels of media use and political discussion, producing a spurious correlation.

The analyst may possess a theoretical framework that suggests the causal order linking two variables. However, the investigator still treads on dangerous ground whenever causality is inferred from correlational data. Indeed, survey research concerning media effects includes many examples of precisely this sort of hazard. For instance, survey data have shown in some cases that understanding of political events is lower among television viewers than television nonviewers. When an assumption of causal order is invoked to account for this correlation, the result is a rather tortured conclusion: where all else is equal, watching television somehow weakens our understanding of political affairs (e.g., Clarke and Fredin 1978; Robinson and Levy 1986). From this perspective, television acts like a vacuum, drawing awareness of political affairs from the minds of its viewers. Or, at minimum, television somehow misleads or bewilders its viewers, leaving them confused about what they have just seen on the news. During the third presidential debate in 1992, Ross Perot suggested that a "giant sucking sound" was the result of U.S. jobs flowing to Mexico. Research on media effects supports an alternative hypothesis; the sound Perot identified may be the result of political knowledge pouring from the brains of the millions of Americans who followed the presidential campaign on television.

My intention is not to belittle the contributions of survey methods, but rather to recognize those methods' fundamental limitations. Generalizable evidence regarding correlations among variables is certainly valuable. When examining such evidence, we simply must be careful to avoid forming unfounded conclusions about the direction of causality.

The Laboratory Experiment

The laboratory experiment is designed specifically to enable identification of causal relationships. Internal validity results because the laboratory researcher can control the variables of interest. If we wish to determine whether or not television drives knowledge out of the brains of viewers, a very simple experiment would produce relevant evidence. For example, we could measure the political knowledge of 100 individuals, and then randomly assign the participants to two treatment conditions. While one group plays volleyball, sunbathes, or naps, the other would watch televised news. We would then remeasure the political knowledge of all participants, and learn if television does indeed cause a reduction in knowledge levels. Adding a level of methodological sophistication, we might also conduct pre- and posttreatment measures of the barometric pressure in our laboratories to gain physical evidence regarding the purported vacuum power of television.

The Iyengar and Kinder experiments (1987; Iyengar, Peters, and Kinder 1982; Iyengar 1991) demonstrate the valuable findings that may emerge when creative investigators turn to the laboratory to study media effects. Methodologically, what is most valuable is that the experiment enjoys high levels of internal validity. However, laboratory experiments also suffer from important methodological limitations. First, both the manipulations themselves and the laboratory setting add an air of artificiality to the proceedings. Such artificiality inevitably limits the generalizability of results. Meticulous design will minimize the severity of this limitation, but it is safe to say that even in the best of circumstances the laboratory experiment will fall short of the typical opinion survey in external validity. External validity is further compromised when researchers draw participants from unrepresentative populations of convenience.

A second limitation of the laboratory experiment is that some research questions are not easily tailored to fit within the confines of the laboratory. If, for example, we are interested in identifying the electoral consequences of access to newspapers, the laboratory experiment will fail us. It would be exceedingly difficult, if not impossible, to manipulate access to newspapers over the course of an entire general election season. Further, we would not be able to study certain critical questions. For instance, we could not examine the relationship between media access and political discussion if the experiment's participants communicate with discussants who are not themselves participating in our study.

In many instances, our only recourse when faced with the characteristic shortcomings of survey and laboratory research is methodological pluralism. If the survey and the experiment produce consistent results, then we can claim both internal and external validity. Where possible, a superior alternative is to maximize internal and external validity within a single research design. For example, an increasingly popular research technique involves the incorporation of experimental manipulations within public opinion surveys (e.g., Piazza, Sniderman, and Tetlock 1989; Mutz 1992; Mondak 1993a). This approach brings both the control of the experiment and the generalizability of the opinion survey. However, few research questions can be pursued with such a strategy, because only experimental manipulations that are simple and brief can be effectively incorporated into a telephone survey. Laboratory researchers often design elaborate multifaceted experimental manipulations in order to test the finest points of competing theoretical frameworks. Similar precision usually cannot be attained within the narrow confines of the telephone interview. Fortunately, other quasi-experimental techniques merge the respective methodological strengths of survey and experimental research. The approach I take in this study is to capitalize on the existence of unique social conditions that approximate the controlled structure of a laboratory experiment.

Merging Survey and Experiment

Methodologically, this study attempts to combine the characteristic strengths of survey and experimental research while avoiding those methods' respective weaknesses. Pittsburgh's newspaper strike serves as this study's focal point. The method is quite straightforward. Survey data are used to compare the political behavior of voters in the Pittsburgh area with the behavior of voters in a similar metropolitan area, Cleveland, where a major local newspaper was available. Thus, the strike provides the makings of a broad social experiment, and the postelection survey offers the necessary individual-level data.

Several previous studies have examined the implications of newspaper strikes for those papers' readers (Berelson [1949] 1979; Kimball 1959, 1963; Bogart 1989). In each of these studies, surveys were conducted to determine respondents' perceptions regarding the impact of each strike. Respondents were asked whether or not they missed the papers, and whether they substituted alternative media to compensate for the dearth of news. Though these studies provide important data concerning the consequences of a newspaper strike, they do not offer insight regarding the electoral significance of print media. First, the studies did not introduce a quasi-experimental design. That is, rather than comparing the behavior of individuals with and without newspapers, the studies simply asked the opinions of persons in the region affected by each strike. Second, the researchers did not examine political effects. The primary question addressed in these studies was how the strikes influenced media use, not how media use affected political behavior. Further, the newspaper stoppages considered in these earlier studies were much shorter than the 1992 Pittsburgh strike, and did not encompass a presidential election season.

In focusing on the Pittsburgh newspaper strike, this study's simple design potentially overcomes the limitations of more conventional survey research and laboratory experiments. The presence or absence of a major local newspaper resembles an experimental manipulation. Consequently, it may be possible to determine whether access to a newspaper *causes* change in mass political behavior. As we have seen, such internal validity typically is not available when data are drawn from a survey of the mass public. Similarly, actual rather than artificially induced political behavior will be examined, with respondents drawn from the population at large rather than from a population of convenience. These features offer a level of external validity unmatched by most laboratory experiments.

It appears that the strike represents an excellent opportunity for study of the role of news media in U.S. elections. Still, new insight will be produced only if the effort to merge survey and experiment successfully captures the two methods' respective strengths. The pessimist might expect that the attempt to join a survey with an experiment merely will combine the two methods' weaknesses. However, close examination of this study's method and procedure reveal that such pessimism is unwarranted. Although the quasi-experimental design is not without limitation, it does offer unique methodological advantages when compared with more familiar opinion surveys and laboratory experiments.

The Postelection Survey

We have seen that the central methodological strength of survey research is external validity. Because the scientific opinion survey draws respondents from the mass public, the opinions of a seemingly small number of individuals may accurately reflect the political predispositions of the general population. Such external validity distinguishes the opinion survey from the laboratory experiment. However, we should not assume that a study's results are generalizable beyond the sample at hand merely because data are drawn from an opinion survey. Instead, our confidence in any particular opinion survey will hinge on the quality of the study's design and execution. This is especially true here, because data are drawn from two distinct urban regions. Further, data are drawn from six congressional districts to allow comparisons of media effects for presidential, Senate, and U.S. House campaigns.

This study's primary data base is a 107-item postelection survey. The survey was completed by 635 respondents in telephone interviews conducted between November 13 and December 7, 1992. Questions include measures of demographic and political characteristics, vote choice, media use, political discussion, and political knowledge. Interviews were administered and conducted by the University of Pittsburgh's University Center for Social and Urban Research. Respondents were selected through use of a random digit-dialing frame. Participation in the survey was limited to individuals who voted in the 1992 elections, and who live in six specific congressional districts.

Ohio's Cuyahoga County, the Cleveland metropolitan area, includes all or part of four U.S. House districts, as does Pennsylvania's Allegheny County. The survey was designed to produce at least 100 completed interviews from the in-county portion of each of the three congressional districts with the largest populations within Cuyahoga and Allegheny counties. Cuyahoga County includes the entire Tenth and Eleventh Districts, slightly less than half of Ohio's Nineteenth District, and a small portion of Ohio's Thirteenth District. Pennsylvania's Fourteenth and Eighteenth Congressional Districts are located entirely within Allegheny County, as are parts of the Fourth and Twentieth Districts. Ohio's Thirteenth District and Pennsylvania's Fourth District are not included in this study. The number of completed interviews for the six districts from which respondents were drawn ranges from 100 in Ohio's Nineteenth to 113 in Pennsylvania's Twentieth. Cleveland- and Pittsburgh-based media are the dominant sources of news in Cuyahoga and Allegheny counties. Interviewing was not extended to surrounding counties because outlying areas are served by their own media sources, limiting the potential influence of urban media. Additionally, the county-level focus provides a degree of commonality with previous studies of information acquisition and electoral behavior (e.g., Owen 1991; Berelson, Lazarsfeld, and McPhee 1954; Lazarsfeld, Berelson, and Gaudet 1944).

Because an equal number of respondents are drawn from six congressional districts, media effects can be studied for three distinct levels of national electoral politics: presidential, Senate, and House. Many recent studies have applied cognitive theories of political behavior in the study of media effects in presidential campaigns (e.g., Beck 1991; Owen 1991; Popkin 1991; Shapiro et al. 1991). Likewise, other analysts have examined media effects at the subpresidential level (e.g., Clarke and Evans 1983; Vermeer 1987b; Weaver and Drew 1993). Although such election-specific research is of clear importance, a methodological design that allows comparisons across levels of elections is essential if we are to sort general media effects from those effects that operate only in specific electoral contexts (see Clausen et al. 1992).

This study's design necessitated the introduction of relatively complicated sampling and interviewing procedures. Initially, countywide samples sufficient to complete interviewing in Ohio's Tenth and Eleventh Districts and Pennsylvania's Fourteenth and Eighteenth Districts were drawn for the Pittsburgh and Cleveland metropolitan areas. However, these samples did not produce the desired number of completed interviews in Ohio's Nineteenth District, or in Pennsylvania's Twentieth. Again, these districts extend beyond the lines of Cuyahoga and Allegheny counties, and only the in-county portions are included in this study. Therefore, supplementary samples were drawn for these areas. During the actual survey, interviewers screened respondents to ensure that they had voted in the 1992 elections, and that they did not live in ineligible locations.[2] For purposes of simplicity, the 326 interviews completed in Allegheny County will be treated as a single sample, as will the 309 interviews completed in Cuyahoga County. However, it is technically more accurate to view this survey as including six distinct samples, one for each congressional district included in the study. Calculation of the survey's completion rates is complicated by the complexity of the sampling and interviewing structures. The best estimate of the completion rate for the Pittsburgh portion of the survey is 43.4 percent. The comparable rate for the Cleveland portion of the study is 38.9 percent.[3]

Comparison of data from the Cleveland and Pittsburgh portions of the survey provides the central focus of this study's quasi-experimental design. However, although the study's underlying structure is quasi-experimental, data are drawn from random probability samples. Thus, in addition to meeting the essential methodological requirements of experimental study, it is also preferred that the samples accurately reflect their respective parent populations. Use of survey data only brings external validity if we have reason to believe that the opinions of the persons who participated in the survey accurately represent the opinions of the general population. To an extent, this characteristic can be accepted on faith; provided that appropriate survey techniques are employed, we enjoy a level of confidence that the samples are indeed representative of their corresponding populations. Additionally, and more tangibly, the actual election results for the relevant races provide external indicators of the survey's accuracy. Although this study is concerned more with process than with outcome, there would be comfort in evidence that voters included in the survey made electoral choices generally comparable to those made by voters throughout Allegheny and Cuyahoga counties. Such evidence is depicted in table 2.1.

Initially, note that data in table 2.1 reveal that the political preferences of voters in the Pittsburgh area closely match those of voters in Greater Cleveland. For example, Bill Clinton, George Bush, and Ross Perot combined to receive 637,086 votes in Cuyahoga County, and 610,509 votes in Allegheny County, with Clinton winning the two counties by essentially identical margins. Second, comparing sample and population results, it is clear that the samples reflect their parent populations with considerable accuracy. The greatest "error" is in Pennsylvania's Twentieth Congressional District, where survey and population results vary by six percentage points. For all 10 races, the average disparity between sample and population is 3.0 points.[4] Thus, this study's survey offers the potential for a level of external validity unavailable in most laboratory research.

By merging survey and experiment, my objective is to attain high levels of both internal and external validity. The survey's Cleveland and Pittsburgh subsamples were drawn using established scientific procedures, and available external indicators reveal that the survey data comport well with the aggregate 1992 election returns. Of course, unlike the conventional opinion survey, this study is designed to allow quasi-experimental comparison of data from the Cleveland and Pittsburgh subsamples. Thus, the next step in assessing the effort to merge survey and experiment is review of this study's quasi-experimental framework.

The Quasi-Experimental Design

Drawing data from a survey of the general population enables this study to overcome the limits on external validity characteristic of laboratory experiments. Hence, at face value, it appears that this investigation may offer a valuable new perspective regarding the role of news media in U.S. elections. However, this conclusion rests on the assumption that this study captures the benefits of experimental design while avoiding the pitfalls. Such an assumption should not be made lightly. Quasi-experimental research suffers several important limitations compared with the conventional laboratory experiment (Campbell and Stanley 1963). Consequently, this study's methodological limitations must be recognized if results are to be interpreted with appropriate caution.

TABLE 2.1. Sample and Population Election Results

Election	County Results			Survey Results		
	Democratic	Republican	Perot	Democratic	Republican	Perot
Cuyahoga County (Cleveland)						
Presidential	53.0 (337,548)	29.4 (187,186)	17.6 (112,352)	56.3 (160)	27.5 (78)	16.2 (46)
Senate	66.4 (390,743)	33.6 (197,776)		70.8 (194)	29.2 (80)	
10th Dist.	43.2 (103,788)	56.8 (136,433)		43.6 (41)	56.4 (53)	
11th Dist.	77.9 (154,718)	22.1 (43,866)		74.4 (64)	26.2 (22)	
19th Dist.	56.4 (70,709)	43.6 (54,619)		60.4 (58)	39.6 (38)	
Allegheny County (Pittsburgh)						
Presidential	53.1 (324,004)	30.0 (183,035)	16.9 (103,470)	53.4 (165)	29.8 (92)	16.8 (52)
Senate	48.6 (277,191)	51.4 (293,156)		42.8 (128)	57.2 (171)	
14th Dist.	73.0 (165,633)	27.0 (61,311)		72.7 (64)	27.3 (24)	
18th Dist.	38.6 (96,655)	61.4 (154,024)		35.3 (36)	64.7 (66)	
20th Dist.	41.2 (22,425)	58.8 (31,997)		35.2 (37)	64.8 (68)	

Sources: Data from Cuyahoga County Board of Elections; Allegheny County Board of Elections; 1992 Cleveland-Pittsburgh Election Study.

Note: Cell entries are percentages of the major-candidate vote. Actual vote totals are in parentheses. With the exception of Ross Perot, independent candidates received a trivial number of votes in most of the elections examined in this study. An exception is Ohio's Eleventh District, where two independent candidates combined to receive 25,040 votes, or 11.2 percent of the four-candidate total. These candidates received the votes of five survey respondents (5.5 percent of the Eleventh District sample).

If control over variables and random assignment of subjects are the critical components of the experimental design, then a study centered on the Pittsburgh strike quite obviously is not a true experiment. This point is easily seen by considering how this investigation would differ had it actually been conducted within the confines of the laboratory. First, in the conventional laboratory experiment, I would not have capitalized on a preexisting newspaper strike. Instead, variance in access to media coverage would have been a structural feature of the study itself. In short, *I* would have shut down Pittsburgh's newspapers or otherwise manipulated access to media coverage. Second, to help ensure that no extraneous factors influenced the Cleveland versus Pittsburgh comparison, voters would have been randomly assigned to the two treatment conditions. That is, I would have gathered the nearly three million residents of Cuyahoga and Allegheny counties and randomly assigned each individual to one of the two locations.

It would appear to be a reality of social science that the pure laboratory experiment is not always practical. Thus, sometimes the most that we can accomplish is to make do with naturally occurring social conditions that approximate an experimental design. Still, no methodological approach should be accepted simply because it is the best that is available. Instead, we must be confident that the study's limitations do not preclude the emergence of useful new findings. Nothing will be gained if the lack of control over variables and the absence of randomization mean that this study fails to capture the essential flavor of experimental research. However, random assignment of subjects and control over variables are not ends in themselves. Through these techniques, we hope to ensure that subjects do differ with respect to the variable that we have manipulated, and that they do not differ in any other systematic way. Fortunately, progress toward these same objectives can be gained with careful design of the quasi-experimental investigation.

In evaluating this study's quasi-experimental design, the first question is whether the newspaper strike affected voters' media-use patterns. Sometimes, experimental manipulations fail. For example, if the researcher is interested in how the credibility of a message's source influences the extent to which audiences accept the message, the researcher will construct what are presumed to be high- and low-credibility descriptions of the sources' credentials. For instance, the speakers might be described as a high school student and a Nobel Prize winner. This manipulation will only produce insight regarding the question of source effects if the audiences perceive a significant difference in the credibility of the speakers. Thus, the researcher performs a "manipulation check" to make sure that the audiences do indeed perceive the Nobel laureate to be more credible than the high school student. In the current case, we must be sure that media access among voters is influenced by the presence or absence of a major local newspaper.

It might seem self-obvious that the information context will be affected when a region's two major daily newspapers cease publication. However, two factors potentially undercut this assumption. First, newspapers simply may not be important sources of electoral information. For instance, if voters turn to television for campaign news, and rely on newspapers only for horoscopes and comics, then this study's "manipulation" would be unsuccessful. Second, even if newspapers do provide some voters with campaign information, voters may be able to receive that same information from alternative sources when access to major local newspapers is denied. The precise manner in which the Pittsburgh newspaper strike affected media exposure is examined in chapter 3. For now, it is sufficient to note that the strike did produce systematic variance in the media-use patterns of voters in Cuyahoga and Allegheny counties. Hence, the quasi-experimental "manipulation" does enable study of the impact of newspapers on electoral behavior.

The second question in evaluating this study's quasi-experimental framework is whether there are sources of systematic variance in addition to the differing access to news media that distinguish this study's Cleveland and Pittsburgh subsamples. In the laboratory experiment, characteristics of the study's participants will vary, but randomization means that the statistical contribution of such variance will be random error. That luxury is not available here. Cleveland and Pittsburgh *are* different, and it is possible that what makes Cleveland different from Pittsburgh also will produce variance in the political behavior of voters from the two regions. Therefore, unlike the laboratory experiment, this study brings no guarantee that all sources of systematic variance can be identified. However, Cleveland was chosen as the second metropolitan area to be studied because Pittsburgh and Cleveland have much in common culturally, historically, economically, and politically. Such commonality potentially serves to limit the methodological consequences of the absence of randomization. Although the research context does not enjoy the purity of the laboratory, the Cleveland and Pittsburgh samples may be sufficiently comparable to enable meaningful quasi-experimental analysis. Simply put, the objective is de facto randomization.

What are some of the similarities linking Pittsburgh and Cleveland? Historically, Pittsburgh has been recognized as the nation's leading producer of steel, whereas Cleveland has been significant in the production of both steel and automobiles. Thus, although their economies have undergone substantial change in recent decades, these "rust belt" cities share historical reputations as two of the nation's major industrial centers. Because the steel and automobile industries provided employment for large numbers of immigrants, Pittsburgh and Cleveland also share strong ethnic identities. In particular, both regions are populated with many individuals of Eastern European ancestry. This shared ethnic heritage has produced many cultural similarities in the neighborhoods of Cleveland and Pittsburgh.

Anecdotal evidence of similarities between Cleveland and Pittsburgh abounds, but does not provide satisfactory proof that the goal of de facto randomization has been met. Instead, systematic and objective evidence is required. We have already seen that voting in the 1992 presidential election was nearly identical in Cuyahoga and Allegheny counties. Data in table 2.1 show that virtually the same number of citizens voted for president in the two counties, and that there is striking similarity in the distribution of votes among the top three candidates. Additional systematic demonstration that Cleveland and Pittsburgh are comparable will proceed on two levels. First, demographic characteristics of the two regions will be examined. Second, individual-level characteristics of respondents in this study's Cleveland and Pittsburgh subsamples will be compared.

Table 2.2 reports demographic data for Cuyahoga and Allegheny counties. These data reveal several similarities between the regions. Nearly equal numbers of persons reside in the two counties, although data in the last two rows of table 2.2 indicate that the Cleveland metropolitan area, which extends beyond the boundaries of Cuyahoga County, is somewhat larger than the Pittsburgh metropolitan area. Also, Cuyahoga and Allegheny counties both experienced a substantial decline in population between 1980 and 1990. Data regarding the size of a region's population are important for understanding both the allocation of U.S. House districts and the dynamics of local media coverage. Further, the size of an urban area largely determines its political wants and needs. Thus, there is comfort in the knowledge that Cuyahoga and Allegheny counties are nearly identical in size, and that the counties have weathered population declines of comparable magnitude. Table 2.2's economic data also reveal substantial similarity, with Cleveland scoring marginally higher than Pittsburgh on both unemployment and per capita income. Likewise, educational attainment is comparable in the two regions. Education levels are slightly higher in Allegheny County, where the University of Pittsburgh is the region's largest employer.

Unfortunately, there is no fixed answer to the question "how close is close enough?" Cuyahoga and Allegheny counties are comparable in size, economic performance, and educational attainment. A glaring disparity on any of these characteristics would have been cause for concern, because each of these factors may influence individual-level political behavior. It remains uncertain whether the objective of de facto randomization has been achieved, but it is clear that several potential stumbling points have been navigated successfully.

A second body of evidence regarding the comparability of the Cleveland and Pittsburgh regions emerges from this study's postelection survey. Political and demographic characteristics of the Cleveland and Pittsburgh respondents are summarized in table 2.3. With one exception, there are no statistically significant differences for the Pittsburgh and Cleveland data. Indeed, the samples exhibit remarkable similarity across a wide range of characteristics. Functionally, this similarity means that de facto randomization did occur for a wealth of demographic and political variables. The one exception to this conclusion, sex, is hardly troubling. It is not the case, as table 2.2 confirms, that the two regions differ so greatly in actuality on this factor. Further, although a higher portion of the survey's

TABLE 2.2. Demographic Characteristics of Cuyahoga and Allegheny Counties

	Cuyahoga County	Allegheny County
Population (1990)	1,412,140	1,336,449
Population rank among counties nationally (1990)	17	19
Population change, 1980–90	-5.8%	-7.8%
Rank among urban counties in rate of population loss, 1980–90	6	3
Percentage female (1990)	53.0	53.1
Unemployment rate (1990)	4.8%	4.2%
Per capita personal income (1989)	19,722	19,249
Persons age 25 and older with at least high school diploma (1990)	74.0%	79.0%
Persons age 25 and older with at least bachelor's degree (1990)	20.1%	22.6%
Population, metropolitan area (1990)	2,759,823	2,242,798
Population rank among metropolitan areas nationally (1990)	13	19

Sources: Slater and Hall 1992; U.S. Department of Commerce 1992a, 1992b.

respondents are female in Cleveland than in Pittsburgh, sex is the one characteristic for which sampling *was* random; thus, the regional disparity arguably represents nothing more than the luck of the draw.[5] Overall, although the research context may not enjoy the purity of the laboratory, the Cleveland and Pittsburgh data are sufficiently comparable to enable

TABLE 2.3. Demographic and Political Characteristics of Cuyahoga County and Allegheny County Respondents

Variable	Scale		Cuyahoga County	Allegheny County
Age	Age in years	Mean	48.59	47.25
		SD	17.54	16.16
		N	301	323
Sex	0 = male,	% female	67.3	57.8[*]
	1 = female	*N*	306	325
Education	0 = grade school	Mean	3.75	3.62
	or less to 7 =	SD	1.70	1.70
	graduate degree	*N*	304	322
Income	0 = under $10,000	Mean	2.97	3.14
	to 7 = $100,000	SD	1.90	1.94
	and over	*N*	256	300
Party ID	0 = strong	Mean	3.72	3.43
	Republican to	SD	2.19	2.34
	6 = strong	*N*	304	320
	Democrat			
Strong	1 = strong	% strong	43.1	47.2
partisan	partisan, 0 =	*N*	304	320
	other			
Ideology	0 = strong	Mean	2.84	2.79
	conservative to	SD	1.94	1.94
	6 = strong	*N*	293	312
	liberal			
Strong	1 = strong, 0 =	% strong	24.2	24.3
ideology	other	*N*	293	312
Civics	0 to 4, no. of	Mean	2.61	2.56
knowledge	civics items	SD	1.21	1.23
	answered	*N*	305	325
	correctly			

[*] Pittsburgh and Cleveland scores significantly different at $p < .05$.

meaningful quasi-experimental analysis. Access to a major local newspaper is the single factor that most clearly differentiates respondents in the Cleveland and Pittsburgh subsamples.[6]

A final question in assessing this study's quasi-experimental design concerns the particular elections contested in Cuyahoga and Allegheny counties in 1992. Because voters in Cleveland and Pittsburgh faced different electoral choices, the races themselves complicate this investigation's quasi-experimental structure. The presidential election presents no difficulty, because the candidates were the same for all of the survey's respondents. However, this study's eight congressional races require closer examination.

The Elections

Although the precise characteristics of the particular elections included in this study are not of direct importance for examination of information acquisition, some background is warranted. In Ohio, incumbent John Glenn, a Democrat, became the first Ohio senator elected to a fourth consecutive term when he defeated Republican challenger Michael DeWine, Ohio's lieutenant governor. Ultimately, the race proved to be Glenn's most challenging. Statewide, Glenn defeated DeWine by a margin of 51 percent to 42 percent, although Glenn fared better in Cuyahoga County than in Ohio as a whole. The campaign was highly contentious. DeWine, who was known as "DeWhine" during his tenure in the U.S. House, launched numerous controversial attacks against Glenn. For example, DeWine, who had used a series of deferments to avoid military service during the Vietnam War, openly (and some would say unwisely) questioned the patriotism of Glenn, who was a renowned fighter pilot during the Korean War prior to joining the nation's fledgling space program. DeWine tried for the Senate again in 1994, running for the seat vacated by Democrat Howard Metzenbaum. This time, DeWine was successful, defeating Metzenbaum's son-in-law, Joel Hyatt.

Republican Arlen Specter, Pennsylvania's incumbent senator, successfully weathered the challenge of Democrat Lynn Yeakel. Specter, who received 50 percent and 56 percent of the vote in his first two senate elections, appeared vulnerable in 1992. Yeakel, a political newcomer, was prompted to enter the race by Specter's treatment of Anita Hill during the Senate Judiciary Committee's hearings concerning the Clarence Thomas Supreme Court nomination. However, Yeakel's campaign stumbled repeatedly, and Yeakel ultimately failed to carry even Allegheny County, a Democratic stronghold (see Hansen 1994).

Among the three U.S. House races in Ohio are one in which a 24-

year veteran Democratic incumbent won comfortably (Louis Stokes, in Ohio's Eleventh District), and one in which a Democratic incumbent with 16 years of service was soundly defeated (Mary Rose Oakar, in Ohio's Tenth District). The Tenth District includes part of Cleveland and suburbs to the west. The Eleventh District also includes part of Cleveland and suburbs to the east. The incumbents, Oakar and Stokes, were both heavily involved in the 1992 House banking scandal (213 overdrafts for Oakar, 551 for Stokes), but only Oakar suffered at the polls. Stokes easily defeated Republican Beryl Rothschild, the mayor of a Cleveland suburb. Oakar was ousted by Republican challenger Martin Hoke, a businessman who moved to the Tenth District to run for Congress. In February 1995, a federal grand jury indicted Oakar on seven felony counts, including charges related to her use of the House bank and to the financing of her 1992 campaign. Ohio's Nineteenth District, the home of Cleveland's most distant suburbs, was an open seat in 1992. The election was won by Democrat Eric Fingerhut, a member of the Ohio state senate. Fingerhut defeated Republican Robert Gardner, a county commissioner in Lake County, Cuyahoga County's neighbor to the northeast. Fingerhut's congressional career was brief, however, as he was a victim of the Republican sweep in 1994.

The Pennsylvania congressional contests also include one in which a Democratic incumbent was reelected with relative ease. William Coyne, a 12-year veteran, gained reelection in Pennsylvania's Fourteenth District by defeating Republican challenger Byron King. The Fourteenth District includes the entire city of Pittsburgh, and several surrounding suburbs. Democrat Austin Murphy, the incumbent in Pennsylvania's Twentieth District, also won reelection. Murphy, a 16-year veteran, had appeared vulnerable since a series of ethics violations first emerged in 1987. The 1992 race was decided by fewer than four thousand votes, and Republican challenger Bill Townsend actually carried nearly 60 percent of the vote in Allegheny County. However, Murphy outspent his challenger by a margin of six to one, enabling the incumbent to overcome his defeat in Allegheny County with a strong showing in the district's four rural counties. With his future electoral prospects seemingly bleak, Murphy declined to seek reelection in 1994.

The final race, in Pennsylvania's Eighteenth District, was one of the nation's most unusual. Incumbent Rick Santorum, a conservative Republican, won the seat in 1990 by defeating 14-year Democratic incumbent Doug Walgren. However, redistricting prior to the 1992 election created a seat in which two-thirds of the registered voters are Democrats and only 29 percent are Republicans (the district resembles a backward C surrounding the city of Pittsburgh). Sensing Santorum's likely electoral jeopardy, 12 candidates entered the Democratic primary. The winner? Frank Pecora, a Republican. While sitting and voting as a Republican in the Pennsylvania state senate, Pecora, whom diplomatic analysts might label as opportunistic, ran as a Democrat in the Eighteenth District's primary. Pecora won the primary with 19 percent of the vote. Rather than backing Pecora, Democratic Party leaders attempted to field an alternative candidate as an independent in the general election, only to find that Pennsylvania law prohibits registered partisans from running as independents; a Republican could run as a Democrat, but a Democrat could not run as an independent. Choosing between Santorum and Pecora, a solid majority of the Eighteenth's voters opted for the incumbent, even though he was a Republican. Santorum likely would have faced strong opposition in 1994. Rather than attempting to defend his vulnerable House seat, Santorum instead sought Harris Wofford's seat in the U.S. Senate. In a campaign with two quite ideologically distinct candidates, Santorum won in a close election against the incumbent, Wofford. Santorum's decision to give up his House seat was wise. When the Republicans captured the House in 1994, Pennsylvania's Eighteenth District was one of only a handful nationally that switched from Republican to Democratic control.

Differences among the six House elections are not particularly troubling, because multiple races are included in both the Cleveland and Pittsburgh portions of the study. For example, the fact that Ohio's Nineteenth District was an open seat in 1992 not only sets that election apart from the three Pittsburgh-area contests, but also from the other two Cleveland races. However, one problem is that, as a whole, the candidates in the Cleveland elections outspent their Pittsburgh counterparts. Money generates publicity, and thus the lower level of spending in Pittsburgh may have reduced the attentiveness of the area's voters to their House campaigns. To a large extent, campaign spending is driven by the behavior of challengers; when the challenger is well funded, the incumbent will spend more in response (e.g., Green and Krasno 1988; Jacobson 1980; Krasno, Green, and Cowden 1994). In Ohio's Tenth and Eleventh Districts, the major challengers spent an average of $380,699 in 1992, dwarfing the $136,823 average for the three Pittsburgh districts.

What factors underlie the Cleveland versus Pittsburgh spending gap? House candidates historically have spent more in Cleveland than in Pittsburgh, perhaps reflecting the higher costs associated with a somewhat larger media market. In the period 1980–90, for example, House candidates in Cleveland spent $1.17 for every $1.00 spent in Pittsburgh. This historical disparity clearly does not fully account for the large spending gap in 1992. However, two additional factors can be dismissed. First, no elements of the Cleveland House races uniquely predisposed them toward high levels of spending. Mary Rose Oakar was a vulnerable incumbent in Ohio's Tenth District, and thus it is not surprising that her challenger was well funded. But Rick Santorum and Austin Murphy also were highly vulnerable in defending Pennsylvania's Eighteenth and Twentieth Districts. The incumbents in Ohio's Tenth and Eleventh Districts received an average of 76.5 percent of the vote in 1990, compared with an average of 62.0 percent for the three Pennsylvania districts. Given that prior margins are associated with subsequent challenger spending (Bond, Covington, and Fleisher 1985; Green and Krasno 1988), we should have seen higher levels of challenger spending in Pittsburgh than in Cleveland in 1992, not the opposite. Second, the challengers in Cleveland did not capitalize on an advantage in political experience to raise more money than their Pittsburgh counterparts. The challengers in Ohio's Tenth District and in Pennsylvania's Fourteenth and Twentieth Districts had not held prior political office. Beryl Rothschild, who opposed Louis Stokes in Ohio's Eleventh, was the mayor of a Cleveland suburb. However, such a local office is less advantageous for a congressional campaign than is service in the state legislature (Bond, Covington, and Fleisher 1985; Green and Krasno 1988; Krasno, Green, and Cowden 1994), giving the edge in political experience to the Pittsburgh candidates by virtue of Frank Pecora's tenure in the state senate.

I believe that the spending gap likely was inflated by the Pittsburgh newspaper strike. Just as spending generates publicity, so too does publicity generate revenue. Two of the three Pittsburgh-area incumbents were highly vulnerable, but their challengers struggled to raise money. Had there been newspapers, these challengers most likely would have run stronger campaigns, prompting vigorous defenses from the incumbents. Hence, with newspapers, the Pittsburgh versus Cleveland spending gap probably would have been reduced. Therefore, at least for the U.S. House races, we are left with a viable quasi-experimental framework.

Unfortunately, the two U.S. Senate races are more problematic. With only one race per region, it will not be possible to demonstrate conclusively that differences between Cleveland and Pittsburgh are attributable to media access rather than to alternative characteristics of the two elections. This point is particularly noteworthy given the relative visibility of Pennsylvania's Specter versus Yeakel contest. This race was much closer in Allegheny County than was Ohio's Glenn-DeWine Senate election within Cuyahoga County. Further, Specter and Yeakel combined to spend twice as much money on their campaigns as did Glenn and DeWine, suggesting that the Pennsylvania Senate election may have enjoyed a high level of visibility in the Pittsburgh area despite the absence of local newspapers.[7]

Conclusion

Great care has been exercised in merging the experiment with the survey so that the methodological strengths of each approach can be accrued. Survey researchers generally do not enjoy any level of control over their independent variables, meaning that conclusive identification of causal rather than correlational effects is rare. Conversely, laboratory research typically cannot induce sweeping effects comparable to shutting down the major newspapers in a large metropolitan area, and experimentalists often possess little evidence regarding the generalizability of their findings. This study's methodological approach does much to overcome these characteristic shortcomings. Because data are drawn from a large-scale public-opinion survey, this study's external validity exceeds that of the conventional laboratory experiment. Further, internal validity is gained because the Cleveland and Pittsburgh respondents experienced very different levels of access to local newspapers, meaning that it will be possible to determine whether or not variance in media exposure *causes* variance in mass political behavior. However, as we have seen, this study's quasi-experimental strategy also brings its own stumbling points, requiring caution in the interpretation of results. Still, by combining the control of the experiment with the representativeness of the public-opinion survey, this study offers a unique opportunity to examine the importance of newspapers in U.S. elections.

CHAPTER 3

Media Exposure

You know that I'll miss you
But strangely I'm glad
Gonna make it without you
And that's what's so sad
— Melanie Safka

This study's quasi-experimental "manipulation" is the Pittsburgh newspaper strike. Because local newspapers were not available in Pittsburgh during the 1992 campaign season, Cleveland versus Pittsburgh comparisons will contrast the political behavior of voters with high versus low levels of access to news coverage of the 1992 elections. These quasi-experimental tests potentially will reveal how media exposure affects voters' knowledge levels, interpersonal discussion, and electoral decision making. However, we should not simply assume that the newspaper strike limited the media exposure of Pittsburgh-area voters. Instead, the success of the experimental manipulation must be verified empirically. If the strike had no impact on media-use patterns in Pittsburgh, then this study offers no unique opportunity to examine the relationship between news media and information acquisition. In other words, if the quasi-experimental manipulation failed to induce variance in voters' access and exposure to news media, then this study will not produce new insight regarding the electoral significance of local newspapers.

My objective in this chapter is to identify the impact of the newspaper strike on the media exposure of Pittsburgh-area voters. Specifically, we will consider the extent to which the strike affected three aspects of media exposure: (1) which media sources voters turned to for news regarding the presidential, Senate, and House elections; (2) the amount of information voters received from local newspapers; and (3) voters' levels of attentiveness to news concerning the 1992 campaigns. Because findings will provide an essential foundation for the quasi-experimental tests to be conducted in later chapters, much of this chapter's analysis resembles the manipulation checks that follow laboratory experiments. Proof that the newspaper strike altered media exposure will establish that subsequent comparisons of the Pittsburgh and Cleveland data are valid tests of the impact of news media on electoral behavior.

Although it is essential to demonstrate that the newspaper strike affected media exposure, this chapter's significance extends beyond the methodological technicality of the manipulation check. First, simultaneous examination of presidential and subpresidential campaigns will reveal whether the importance of particular media sources varies for different electoral contexts. Do voters tailor the information search on a campaign-specific basis, or do they rely on a generic information base for a multitude of elections? Second, study of how Pittsburgh voters adapted to the absence of newspapers will fuel discussion of both the rationality and the flexibility of the American voter. For example, evidence that voters actively endeavored to find viable substitutes for their local newspapers would support a relatively optimistic evaluation of electoral decision making.

In chapter 2, we saw that the quasi-experimental design fails to capture in full the characteristic strengths of the laboratory experiment. Here, in contrast, we will see that this study also enjoys certain advantages over more conventional laboratory studies. In the laboratory, manipulation of media exposure can produce very revealing findings regarding the nature of media effects. What is missing, however, is the real-world flavor of information acquisition. With a quasi-experimental design, voters are allowed to respond to a sweeping change in the information context any way they see fit. Hence, the strike enables a glimpse at the actual dynamics of information acquisition, an advantage unmatched by traditional laboratory experiments.

Prior to examining data relevant to the question of media exposure, it is useful to consider what types of effects the newspaper strike may have had on information acquisition. Broadly, two types of effects are possible. First, and most obvious, the strike may have limited the amount of information voters acquired from local newspapers. If no such effect emerges, then the quasi-experimental manipulation fails. The strike will not have affected the amount of campaign information voters received from newspapers if newspapers have no role in electoral politics, or if Pittsburgh voters turned to alternative newspapers to replace the two major dailies. Second, if the strike did decrease voters' access to information from local newspapers, then it is also possible that the strike reduced the general level of media exposure. This effect would emerge if voters did not receive information from local newspapers, and did not locate alternative media sources to fill the information vacuum. Conversely, there will be no impact on general levels of media exposure if voters substituted information from broadcast media, alternative print media, or social networks, to fill the void caused by the newspaper strike.

The possible insight this study can produce depends entirely on how Pittsburgh's newspaper strike influenced media exposure. Table

3.1 summarizes three possible scenarios. First, if the strike reduced neither the amount of information voters received from newspapers nor overall levels of media exposure, then the quasi experiment will collapse. Second, if the strike affected the amount of information provided by newspapers, but not total media exposure, then quasi-experimental tests can pursue whether or not newspapers play a unique role in U.S. elections. Under this scenario, we would find that Cleveland and Pittsburgh respondents differ on the quantity of information received from local newspapers, but do not differ on the overall quantity of information received from news media, or on levels of attentiveness to the news. This scenario would allow tests showing whether it matters which media source informs the voter. For example, do voters learn more about candidates' policy positions from local newspapers than from broadcast media?

The third scenario arises if the newspaper strike reduced the total amount of information voters received from news media. In this setting, quasi-experimental tests can address the broad electoral significance of media. In short, does electoral behavior change if the voter resides in a media-rich rather than a media-poor decision-making context? Provided that the strike had any effect on the media-use patterns of Pittsburgh's voters, the strike facilitates study of either the *unique* role of local

TABLE 3.1. Possible Effects of the Pittsburgh Newspaper Strike

Effect on Information Received from Local Newspapers	Effect on Media Exposure	Explanation	Implication
No effect	No effect	Either newspapers have no role in electoral politics, or Pittsburgh voters found other newspapers to replace the major dailies	"Manipulation" fails; quasi-experimental tests cannot be conducted
Reduction in information	No effect	Strike limited access to newspapers, but voters replaced newspapers with other media sources	Quasi-experimental tests can determine if newspapers play a unique electoral role, but cannot detect general media effects
Reduction in information	Reduction in information	Strike limited access to newspapers, and voters did not replace newspapers with other media sources	Quasi-experimental tests can measure general media effects

newspapers or the *general* role of news media. Further, because media exposure will be examined on an election-specific basis, it is possible that the newspaper strike will enable different types of quasi-experimental tests for the presidential and subpresidential campaigns.

The first step in evaluating the impact of the strike is to determine which media sources voters in Pittsburgh and in Cleveland turned to for news about the 1992 elections. Later, we will consider how much information voters received, and how attentive voters were to the news.

Sources of Campaign Information

The importance of newspapers as sources of electoral information is not self-obvious. Generally, a strong majority of Americans report that television is their primary source of news (Roper 1983; Miller, Singletary, and Chen 1988), raising the possibility that local newspapers do not contribute to the information base of most voters. However, regardless of the apparent preeminence of television, the local newspaper is far from obsolete (Miller, Singletary, and Chen 1988; Bogart 1984, 1989). Most Americans do read newspapers, and many view television and print as complementary news sources (Bogart 1984, 1989). Additionally, the selection of a news medium may vary for different news topics. Newspapers may be the medium of choice for news about sports, business, and local elections, for instance, whereas television may be the primary source of news about the weather, crime, and the latest fads. Television's role as the nation's primary news source does not preclude the local newspaper from offering a significant contribution to an informed electorate.

In this study's postelection survey, respondents answered three batteries of media-use items, one for each electoral contest. Included were questions designed to identify the most important sources of news for each campaign. For the presidential election, for example, respondents were asked: "Where did you get most of your news about the presidential election; from the radio, from television, from national newspapers, from local newspapers, from magazines, from talking to people, or where?" A follow-up question identified each respondent's second most important source of news. Identical questions are included for the Senate and U.S. House campaigns. Analysis of results for these items is the first step in determining how Pittsburgh's newspaper strike affected media exposure.

Sources of News for the Presidential Campaign

Generally, television news reports do not possess the characteristic depth and precision of newspaper stories. However, the presidential campaign may be an exception. Television devotes enormous effort to coverage of presidential elections. In 1992, for example, CNN and the national broadcast networks aired hundreds of hours of special programs and campaign reports, with substantial collective detail. The quality of televised reports concerning the presidential campaign may be debated (e.g., Patterson and McClure 1976; Patterson 1980), but their quantity could hardly be more daunting. Such extensive coverage may leave little room for newspapers to offer a truly unique contribution. Consequently, the electoral role of local newspapers may be far more ambiguous for presidential campaigns than for other news events, including subpresidential elections. Similarly, in reporting on the presidential campaign, local newspapers must compete against alternative print media—news magazines and national newspapers. Hence, even if the voter prefers print media, the local newspaper will not necessarily be the medium of choice.

Ultimately, the relative significance of the local newspaper is dictated by the preferences of the news consumer. If voters rely on local newspapers for information about the presidential campaign, then those newspapers *are* important. The preferences of the Cleveland and Pittsburgh respondents are depicted in table 3.2.

In both Cuyahoga and Allegheny counties, television is the overwhelming first choice for news about the presidential campaign. Nearly 70 percent of respondents list television as their top source of news for the presidential race, and nearly 90 percent report television to be either their first or second choice. In the Cleveland area, local newspapers are a distant second, but also a strong second; over 65 percent of respondents from Cuyahoga County list local papers as one of their top two sources. No other medium scores among the top two sources for even 20 percent of respondents. Further, many voters apparently view television and the local newspaper as complements. For example, 87 percent of respondents who included local newspapers among their top two choices paired newspapers with television. In the presidential campaign, newspapers may play a supporting role to television, but the Cleveland data suggest that this role is far from trivial.

Denied access to a major local paper, voters in Allegheny County appear to have turned to a variety of alternative news sources. In particular, radio, magazines, and national newspapers show clear gains versus Cuyahoga County. Despite the newspaper strike, some voters still report reliance on local newspapers, an apparent reference to the various suburban publications available in Allegheny County, particularly the Greensburg *Tribune-Review* and the *North Hills News Record*. However, it is clear that the Pittsburgh strike did cause a substantial reduction in the role of the local newspaper. This finding paves the way for quasi-experimental tests of the impact of local newspapers on information acquisition. Also, although reliance on television in Pittsburgh is up slightly over the Cleveland area, there appears to be a ceiling on television use. That is, it seems that some voters will *not* draw on television as a source of news about the presidential campaign, even when the most likely alternative, the local newspaper, is unavailable. This point comports well with Bogart's (1989) finding that New York City residents did not flock to television as an alternative news source during a 1978 newspaper strike. It may be that some voters do not turn to television because they refuse to go without print; 55 percent of Pittsburgh-area respondents report selecting a print medium as their first or second source of news about the presidential campaign. Ultimately, voters in Pittsburgh *did* find replacements for their missing newspapers; very few respondents were unable to name two sources of electoral news. Of course, simply naming two sources does not mean that Pittsburgh voters

TABLE 3.2. Sources of Information, the Presidential Campaign

	First Source of Information		Second Source of Information	
	Cuyahoga County	Allegheny County	Cuyahoga County	Allegheny County
Television	63.4	72.7	23.3	17.8
Local newspapers	19.4	4.3	46.9	14.4
Radio	4.9	8.0	12.0	22.7
Talking to people	4.5	0.9	3.2	9.8
Magazines	3.2	5.5	5.5	10.4
National newspapers	2.6	7.7	3.6	17.2
Other	1.3	0.6	2.3	2.5
Don't know/ no second source	0.6	0.3	3.2	5.2
N	309	326	309	326

Note: Cell entries are column percentages.

received information comparable in quantity or quality to that received by Cleveland voters.

This descriptive exercise leaves many questions unanswered. For example, does the propensity of Cleveland voters to select particular media sources vary as a systematic function of individual-level political or demographic characteristics? Most importantly, does the relative ease of reliance on television mean that television is selected for its efficiency rather than its quality? The apparent ceiling on television use may imply that some exposure to television news is accidental, whereas exposure to print media requires deliberate effort. If this is the case, we should find that respondents with high levels of civic concern and political interest are least likely to select television as their primary source of news about the presidential campaign (see Miller, Singletary, and Chen 1988; Clarke and Fredin 1978; Owen 1991). Similarly, are there specific traits that affect the likelihood that respondents from the Pittsburgh area will replace local newspapers with one medium rather than another?

To pursue these questions, a multinomial logistic regression model will be estimated. The dependent variable is the respondent's self-reported first source of information about the presidential campaign. Data from table 3.2 will be collapsed into five categories: (1) radio; (2) television; (3) local newspapers; (4) national print media (from table 3.2, magazines and national newspapers); and (5) other (from table 3.2, talking to people, other, and don't know). Later, similar models will be estimated with data concerning the Senate and House campaigns. A parsimonious modeling strategy is followed for two reasons. First, multinomial logit models defy easy interpretation. Logit models are inherently interactive, because the impact of a particular independent variable will differ across the values of all other independent variables. Consequently, model interpretation becomes extremely complex when numerous independent variables are included. Second, the similarity of the Cleveland and Pittsburgh subsamples demonstrated in chapter 2 means that there is no need to include superfluous control variables. Indeed, "over-control" can adversely affect estimation of the impact of the manipulation in a quasi-experimental design (Achen 1986).

The multinomial logit model includes three independent variables: a dummy variable distinguishing the Cleveland and Pittsburgh respondents (coded 1 if Pittsburgh, 0 if Cleveland), a measure of civics knowledge (coded 0 to 4, the number of civics items answered correctly), and a Pittsburgh × civics knowledge interaction term. Zaller (1992) demonstrates that civics knowledge is superior to education, self-reported political interest, and several other alternatives as a general measure of political awareness. The four items used in this analysis are drawn from Delli

Carpini and Keeter's (1993) extensive study of several dozen knowledge items. Here, the measure of civics knowledge provides a simple means to determine if the voter's medium of choice varies as a function of political attentiveness. The four knowledge questions, and the percentage of respondents answering each correctly, are:

Was Former President Franklin Roosevelt a Democrat or a Republican? (78.2)

What are the first 10 amendments in the Constitution called? (58.7)

Whose responsibility is it to determine if a law is constitutional or not? Is it the responsibility of the president, the Congress, or the Supreme Court? (71.4)

How much of a majority is required for the Senate and the House to override a presidential veto? (50.2)

Table 3.3 depicts the results of the multinomial logit estimation procedure. The multinomial logit technique contrasts one response category, in this case radio, with each of the other choices. The coefficients for particular paired contrasts are not as important as the total impact of each independent variable. In table 3.3, the chi-square statistics for the independent variables indicate the effect that occurs when each variable

TABLE 3.3. Multinomial Logistic Regression Results: Sources of Information about the Presidential Campaign

	Radio vs. Television	Radio vs. Local Papers	Radio vs. National Print Media	Radio vs. Other
Constant	2.812	1.138	-1.384	0.902
Pittsburgh	0.261	-1.475	0.297	-0.956
	Variable chi-square = 55.727 ($p < .001$)			
Civics knowledge	-0.097	0.079	0.523	-0.247
	Variable chi-square = 35.620 ($p < .001$)			
Pittsburgh × civics knowledge	-0.233	-0.180	-0.013	-0.332
	Variable chi-square = 1.140			
$N = 630$	Model chi-square = 92.487			

is added to the model in a stepwise manner.[1] For example, the 55.727 statistic for the Pittsburgh dummy variable means that a model with this variable outperforms a constant-only model, establishing that media-use patterns do differ by region. This effect provides conclusive evidence that Pittsburgh's newspaper strike substantially altered voters' media-use patterns. The 35.620 chi-square statistic for civics knowledge is also significant, although the 1.140 statistic for the interaction term is not.

Output from multinomial logit models is most easily understood by graphing the predicted probabilities. Figure 1 displays the most important of the estimated probabilities derived from the logit coefficients in table 3.3. Figure 1A provides stark evidence that television and local newspapers formed a dominant duo in Cleveland. However, a strong civics knowledge effect is also apparent. Whereas television is the overwhelming first choice for news for respondents with low levels of civics knowledge, the gap between television and local newspapers closes by over twenty points as knowledge increases. Still, television remains the top source of news about the presidential campaign for respondents at all levels of civics knowledge. Next, note that the gap between television and its competitors is greater in figure 1B than in figure 1A for nearly all respondents. Nevertheless, the essential pattern of results is similar in Pittsburgh and Cleveland. For example, in both Cleveland and Pittsburgh there is only a 58 percent likelihood that television is the first choice for news about the presidential campaign for respondents who scored in the highest category of civics knowledge. Further, the propensity for reliance on print media increases as a function of civics knowledge; in both Cleveland and Pittsburgh, there is a greater than 30 percent likelihood that a respondent in the highest category of civics knowledge will rely on print media for news about the presidential campaign. In Cleveland, local newspapers appear to be the print medium of choice. But in Pittsburgh, where access to a major local paper was denied, magazines and national newspapers seemingly functioned as acceptable alternatives.

Although self-reports of media use are limited vehicles for examination of media influence, this analysis suggests two conclusions regarding the relative importance of local newspapers as information sources for the presidential campaign. First, the dominance of television allows local newspapers only a supporting role. Television is the first choice for news about the presidential campaign for a vast majority of respondents. The television versus newspaper choice largely hinges on political awareness, but even voters in the highest category of civics knowledge are more likely to receive news from television than from print sources. Second, those voters who do rely on newspapers appear to do so out of genuine choice

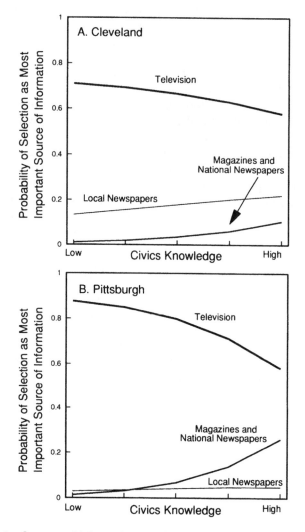

Fig. 1. Sources of information about the 1992 presidential campaign, by civics knowledge. (Data from table 3.3.)

instead of simple convenience. This point is demonstrated by the fact that, absent access to a major local newspaper, many voters in Pittsburgh replaced print with print. Rather than falling back on television or radio, many would-be readers of the local newspaper turned to magazines and national newspapers, producing an effect across civics knowledge mirroring Cleveland's television versus local newspaper pattern.

Sources of News for the Senate Campaign

For the presidential campaign, media-use patterns are largely driven by the role of television; most voters choose television as their primary media source, and the selection of newspapers as a second source possibly reflects a perception that the local newspaper provides a complement to television coverage. In examining the role of media for Senate elections, we know at the outset that the media context differs from that of the presidential campaign. Whereas television's national news networks devote enormous effort to coverage of the presidential campaign, no single state's Senate race receives comparable national attention. Thus, televised reports about the Senate election will be predominantly local rather than national in origin. The informational value of television's coverage of Senate campaigns has been questioned (Clarke and Fredin 1978), yet the role of television from the perspective of the voter still may be substantial. Additionally, national print media will be of far less relevance for the Senate than for the presidential campaign, leaving print-reliant voters no obvious alternative to the local newspaper.

Differences in the media context for the presidential and Senate campaigns will not necessarily affect media-use patterns, and thus may not alter the relative significance of local newspapers. For example, if voters primarily attend to news about the presidential election, and receive news concerning lower races through accidental exposure, then our survey respondents may report the same sources of information for all political contests. Indeed, media-use patterns for the presidential and Senate races will differ only if voters either tailor information acquisition on an election-specific base or perceive the value of particular media sources to vary by election.

Table 3.4 reports the sources of information about the Senate campaign registered by Cleveland and Pittsburgh voters. In Cleveland, television again is the first choice of a majority of respondents. However, the gap separating television and newspapers is far narrower than that reported for the presidential race in table 3.2. Comparing the Cleveland and Pittsburgh data, it is clear that Pittsburgh's newspaper strike affected media-use patterns for the Senate campaign. In response to the local newspaper strike, Pittsburgh voters appear to have drawn primarily on broadcast media for news about the senate campaign; reliance on both television and radio is markedly greater in Pittsburgh than in Cleveland. Residents of Allegheny County who were desirous of print media apparently found little satisfaction in magazines and national newspapers. In contrast, a full 30 percent of these respondents listed local newspapers among their top two media sources, suggesting that Allegheny County's suburban papers were accepted as replacements for the missing major dailies.

Multinomial logit coefficients are reported in table 3.5, and estimated probabilities are depicted in figure 2. Once again, the dependent variable is the self-reported most important source of information. In table 3.5, the large chi-square statistic for the Pittsburgh dummy variable confirms that media-use patterns for the Senate campaigns differ among voters in Pittsburgh and Cleveland. Turning to figure 2A, the estimates reveal that among Cleveland voters television and local newspapers dominated information acquisition for the Senate race even more so than for the presidential campaign. To some extent, this heightened importance is to be expected, due to the minimal relevance of national print media for a statewide electoral contest. For respondents with the lowest levels of civics knowledge, the relative significance of television and local newspapers matches that for the presidential race, as shown in figure 1. However, media use for the Senate campaign changes dramati-

TABLE 3.4. Sources of Information, the Senate Campaign

	First Source of Information		Second Source of Information	
	Cuyahoga County	Allegheny County	Cuyahoga County	Allegheny County
Television	52.9	66.3	28.9	20.7
Local newspapers	33.1	10.2	36.4	19.8
Radio	3.6	12.1	16.6	23.2
Talking to people	3.6	2.5	4.2	8.7
Magazines	1.0	1.9	1.6	5.3
National newspapers	1.3	1.2	3.6	8.4
Other	2.6	1.2	2.9	3.4
Don't know/ no second source	1.9	1.2	2.9	5.6
N	308	323	308	323

Note: Cell entries are column percentages.

cally across civics knowledge. Most importantly, the lines depicting the estimated likelihood that respondents will be primarily reliant on television and local newspapers virtually converge for respondents with the highest levels of political awareness. Thus, it appears that local newspapers function as something more than a complement to television, representing the news medium of choice for a substantial subgroup of voters.

The results depicted in figure 2B provide stark evidence of the effect of Pittsburgh's newspaper strike. Across all levels of civics knowledge, Pittsburgh voters were only about one-fourth as likely to rely on local newspapers for news about the Senate campaign as were voters in Cleveland. However, unlike in the presidential election, national print media did little to fill the void. Even among the most knowledgeable respondents, the likelihood of reliance on national print media falls short of 0.15. This finding, coupled with the high probability estimates for television, suggests that televised news may have won the attentiveness of many voters by default. The scores for television use in Pittsburgh exceed those in Cleveland by 13 points or more for all voters except those who received perfect marks on the civics knowledge measure.

A comparison of media use for the presidential and Senate campaigns indicates that the importance of particular media sources varies

TABLE 3.5. Multinomial Logistic Regression Results: Sources of Information about the Senate Campaign

	Radio vs. Television	Radio vs. Local Papers	Radio vs. National Print Media	Radio vs. Other
Constant	2.937	1.826	-0.336	1.098
Pittsburgh	-0.333	-1.741	-2.751	-0.791
	Variable chi-square = 68.497 ($p < .001$)			
Civics knowledge	-0.099	0.140	-0.045	-0.093
	Variable chi-square = 22.147 ($p < .001$)			
Pittsburgh × civics knowledge	-0.244	-0.229	0.806	-0.301
	Variable chi-square = 6.276			
$N = 630$	Model chi-square = 96.920			

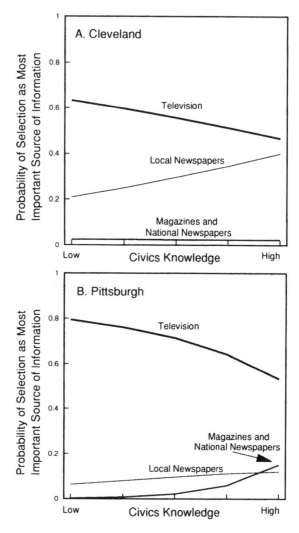

Fig. 2. Sources of information about the 1992 Senate campaign, by civics knowledge. (Data from table 3.5.)

both as a function of characteristics of the voters, and by electoral contest. Thus far, television appears to be the preeminent source of campaign information. However, local newspapers rival television among voters with higher levels of political awareness, especially for the Senate campaign. The behavior of those voters deprived of access to a major local newspaper also has been revealing. For the presidential race, where alternative print media were available, would-be newspaper readers accepted other print sources as substitutes. However, the ability of voters to replace the local newspaper as an information source may be limited; for the Senate race, the most common approach to information acquisition among the erstwhile newspaper-reliant was simply to fall back on television.

Sources of News for the House Campaign

Extensive coverage of U.S. House campaigns is not a winning strategy for the television or radio station concerned with garnering high ratings. The problem is not that listeners and viewers are uninterested in congressional elections, but that any interest that does exist likely will be limited to only that news pertaining to the voter's own congressional district. Consider the Cleveland area, where parts of four congressional districts are included in Cuyahoga County, and additional districts fall within the boundaries of the broadcast region. When a Cleveland television or radio station airs a news story focusing on a single congressional race, that story will be of little or no relevance for at least three out of four prospective audience members. Hence, the need to avoid alienating its audience constitutes a disincentive for the broadcast news organization to devote air time to congressional campaigns.[2] To some extent, major local newspapers face the same market concerns. However, the newspaper reader can turn the page until an item of interest is found, but the television and radio audience must escape the news broadcast entirely in order to escape an unengaging story. Thus, the need to report stories of widespread appeal is greater for broadcast media than for print media.

Regardless of the incentive structure faced by broadcast news organizations, the possibility remains that a sizable portion of the electorate relies primarily on television or radio for news concerning congressional campaigns. Where the voter has less interest, the voter will exert less effort. Therefore, if the House election fails to spark intrigue, then many voters may be content to process only that information that comes with little or no cost. In short, the information needs of the boundedly rational voter may conflict with the profit structure of broadcast media, and thus access to "easy" information may be the most limited in precisely those electoral contests where its utility potentially could be the greatest. Media deluge voters with information pertaining to the presidential election, a campaign in which voters as a whole probably would be willing to seek out information if it were not so readily available. In contrast, media coverage of House elections is relatively scarce, meaning that the disinterested voter may be forced to get by with extremely little campaign-specific information. Hence, rational behavior on the part of media and rational behavior on the part of the electorate potentially combine to form a less than optimal end. The dominance of the presidential campaign may come at the expense of important subnational elections.

Table 3.6 depicts the sources of information reported by the Cleveland and Pittsburgh respondents. In Cuyahoga County, television again emerges as the medium of choice, although the gap separating television and local newspapers has narrowed compared with results for the presidential and Senate campaigns. Interestingly, over one-third of Allegheny County respondents report reliance on local newspapers despite the lack of access to a major daily. Two factors likely contribute to this curious result. First, those voters who sought information about the House elections simply had little choice. Coverage by television and radio was minimal, and other alternatives were essentially nonexistent. Note, for example, that nearly 15 percent of Pittsburgh-area respon-

TABLE 3.6. Sources of Information, the House Campaign

	First Source of Information		Second Source of Information	
	Cuyahoga County	Allegheny County	Cuyahoga County	Allegheny County
Television	47.5	57.9	34.8	20.6
Local newspapers	34.4	15.5	35.4	19.0
Radio	6.2	11.1	13.1	25.3
Talking to people	4.3	4.1	6.6	7.0
Magazines	2.0	1.9	0.7	3.2
National newspapers	1.0	1.6	2.6	5.47
Other	3.0	4.4	2.0	4.7
Don't know/ no second source	3.0	4.4	4.9	14.9
N	305	316	305	316

Note: Cell entries are column percentages.

dents were unable to name two information sources. Second, the county's suburban papers did cover the U.S. House elections in some detail, providing voters with viable substitutes for the major papers. Still, reliance on broadcast media is much higher in Pittsburgh than in Cleveland, suggesting that many voters may have fallen back on free media rather than actively searching for relevant print coverage.

Multinomial logit results for the House data are limited to four categories; because so few respondents relied on national print media for news about the congressional elections, those sources are included in the "other" grouping. Coefficient estimates are reported in table 3.7, and probability estimates are graphed in figure 3. In Cleveland, we see that civics knowledge largely drives the selection of television or the local newspaper as the primary news source. In figure 3A, the lines depicting the estimated probabilities for television and local newspapers intersect for respondents with the highest level of civics knowledge. Reliance on television also diminishes across civics knowledge in Pittsburgh, as seen in figure 3B. Still, the large gap between television and its competitors suggests that the newspaper strike forced many Pittsburgh residents to fall back on television for news about the local congressional campaigns. Analysis of media-use data for the presidential, Senate, and

TABLE 3.7. Multinomial Logistic Regression Results: Sources of Information about the House Campaign

	Radio vs. Television	Radio vs. Local Papers	Radio vs. Other
Constant	2.885	2.049	1.005
Pittsburgh	-0.386	-1.578	-0.668
	Variable chi-square = 31.864 ($p < .001$)		
Civics knowledge	-0.327	-0.124	-0.130
	Variable chi-square = 14.803 ($p < .01$)		
Pittsburgh × civics knowledge	0.004	0.076	0.130
	Variable chi-square = 0.452		
N = 616	Model chi-square = 47.120		

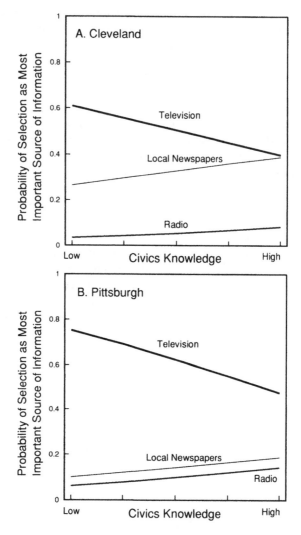

Fig. 3.   Sources of information about the 1992 House campaign, by civics knowledge. (Data from table 3.7.)

U.S. House elections supports several conclusions. First, and most obvious, Pittsburgh's newspaper strike substantially altered voters' media-use patterns for the presidential, Senate, and U.S. House campaigns. There is great comfort in this conclusion, because it constitutes a positive result for the quasi experiment's critical manipulation check. On a more substantive level, the second conclusion is that voters adapt information acquisition on an election-specific basis. Voters apparently perceive the electoral functions of media sources to vary by election, and thus respondents choose different primary information sources for different electoral contests. This finding leads to a third obvious conclusion: the relative importance of local newspapers increases for lower-level elections. Among Cleveland voters, reliance on newspapers peaked with the House race, and reached its lowest point for the presidential campaign. Fourth, political awareness functions as a consistent predictor of the propensity for reliance on local newspapers, particularly for sub-presidential elections.

It appears that Pittsburgh-area voters were most successful in adapting to the newspaper strike when seeking alternative sources of information concerning the presidential campaign. Due to the availability of news magazines and national newspapers, those voters who prefer print media had little difficulty in replacing their missing local newspapers. In contrast, information acquisition was more problematic for the Senate and House elections, and no media source emerged as the preferred alternative to the newspaper. This absence of a clear substitute does not mean that voters failed to overcome the strike; examination of media-use patterns alone is insufficient to answer this question. Fortunately, this issue can be pursued through estimation of the amount of information voters received from specific news sources, and through examination of the impact of media access on attentiveness to campaign news.

How Much Information?

Evidence regarding voters' media preferences provides one indication of the relative importance of alternative media sources. However, viewed in isolation, such evidence will be misleading if voters perceive the information value of different media sources to vary. For example, although voters more frequently report television rather than local newspapers to be their top source of electoral news, newspaper-reliant voters may perceive themselves to be better informed than their television-reliant counterparts. Thus, additional insight can be gained through attention to the *amount* of information voters claim to have received from various media sources.

Rather than measuring the quantity of information received from all possible news sources, the postelection survey was designed to allow comparison of local newspapers and broadcast media as information sources. Specifically, survey respondents were asked three questions regarding the quantity of information received from television and radio, and three matching questions focusing on local newspapers:[3]

About how much information would you say you got about the presidential/ Senate/congressional campaign from television and radio—would you say a great deal, some, only a little, or none at all?

And about how much information would you say you got about the presidential/Senate/congressional campaign from local newspapers—would you say a great deal, some, only a little, or none at all?

The results depicted in table 3.8 indicate that voters apparently perceive themselves as being relatively well informed about the 1992 presidential campaign. In Cleveland, for example, nearly 70 percent of respondents report receiving a great deal of information about the presidential campaign from broadcast media, and over 40 percent claim to have received a great deal of information from local newspapers. To an extent, the preeminence of television suggested earlier by the media-use data now seems less overwhelming. In table 3.2, we saw that 3.3

TABLE 3.8. Amount of Information Received from Broadcast Media and Local Newspapers about the 1992 Presidential Campaign

	Broadcast Media		Local Newspapers	
	Cuyahoga County	Allegheny County	Cuyahoga County	Allegheny County
A great deal	211 (68.3)	237 (72.9)	128 (41.4)	20 (6.2)
Some	80 (25.9)	74 (22.8)	126 (40.8)	71 (21.9)
Only a little	14 (4.5)	12 (3.7)	38 (12.3)	92 (28.4)
None at all	4 (1.3)	2 (.6)	17 (5.5)	141 (43.5)
Mean	2.612	2.680	1.858	0.907
N	309	325	309	324
t-value, Cuyahoga vs. Allegheny	-1.419		17.766	

Note: Percentages are in parentheses. Means and t-values are calculated with data coded 3 = a great deal to 0 = none at all.

Cleveland-area voters reported television to be their top source of news about the presidential campaign for every one voter who selected local newspapers (the ratio is 3.5:1 when those respondents selecting television and those selecting radio are summed). In contrast, only 1.6 voters received a great deal of information from broadcast media for every one that received a comparable amount of information from local papers. Thus, although voters most frequently report television to be their top source of news about the presidential campaign, many respondents find the information value of broadcast media and local newspapers to be roughly comparable. This point comports well with previous findings that individuals' self-reports of television as a primary news source tend to overstate the amount of information actually acquired from televised news (Roper Organization 1984; Robinson and Davis 1990).

Not surprisingly, Pittsburgh respondents claim to have received very little information about the presidential race from local newspapers. The gap between Cleveland and Pittsburgh meets the highest standards of statistical significance. Hence, in addition to altering the media-use patterns of area voters, the newspaper strike also brought a substantial reduction in the amount of information voters received about the presidential campaign from local newspapers. Once again, a manipulation check produces positive results, confirming that the strike has created a viable social experiment. Note, however, that the reduction in information from local newspapers is not offset by a corresponding gain in information from broadcast media. Although Pittsburgh respondents do claim to have received slightly more information from television and radio than do Cleveland respondents, the minimal gain falls short of statistical significance.

Senate data are depicted in table 3.9. Comparing the presidential and Senate results, we see that voters claim to have received substantially less information about the Senate campaign than about the presidential election. However, this decline is driven almost entirely by a perceived decrease in the importance of television. In Cleveland, the portion of the sample claiming to have received a great deal of news about the Senate campaign from broadcast media is down over 30 points versus the presidential campaign (68.3 percent vs. 37.7 percent); in contrast, the score for local newspapers declines by only seven points (41.4 percent vs. 33.9 percent). Consequently, the gap between broadcast media and local newspapers essentially vanishes for the Senate campaign. Although most Cleveland respondents reported broadcast media to be their top source of news about Ohio's Senate election, local newspapers strongly challenge broadcast media when we focus on the quantity of information voters received.

Data for Pittsburgh mirror results for the presidential campaign.

The Cleveland versus Pittsburgh gap in the quantity of information obtained from local newspapers reaches essentially identical levels of statistical significance for the presidential and Senate elections. Further, it is the case in both elections that Pittsburgh respondents report a nonsignificant increase in the amount of information received from television and radio. The newspaper strike caused an information void that broadcast media failed to fill.

In table 3.10, we see that the gap between broadcast media and local newspapers among Cleveland voters is completely erased for the House campaigns, where exactly the same number of respondents report receiving a great deal of information from the two media sources. Far fewer respondents report reliance on local newspapers than on television, yet the information value of broadcast media and local newspapers are roughly comparable. Thus, to some extent it seems that the television consumer receives empty calories. As a result, the importance of television relative to local newspapers appears to be less than was suggested by the media-use data, particularly for the U.S. House campaigns.

TABLE 3.9. Amount of Information Received from Broadcast Media and Local Newspapers about the 1992 Senate Campaigns

	Broadcast Media		Local Newspapers	
	Cuyahoga County	Allegheny County	Cuyahoga County	Allegheny County
A great deal	114 (37.7)	144 (44.7)	103 (33.9)	15 (4.7)
Some	144 (47.7)	131 (40.7)	140 (46.1)	67 (20.9)
Only a little	37 (12.3)	38 (11.8)	43 (14.1)	100 (31.3)
None at all	7 (2.3)	9 (2.8)	18 (5.9)	138 (43.1)
Mean	2.209	2.273	1.750	0.872
N	302	322	304	320
t-value, Cuyahoga vs. Allegheny	-1.062		17.231	

Note: Percentages are in parentheses. Means and t-values are calculated with data coded 3 = a great deal to 0 = none at all.

Interestingly, examining results for the congressional campaigns, we see that respondents in Pittsburgh report receiving *less* information from broadcast media than respondents in Cleveland. How could broadcast media fare worse where they are the only game in town? Two explanations seem plausible. First, it may be that the ability of voters to recall where they received information is minimal, but they are highly able to assess the cumulative amount of information they have received. That is, voters know how well informed they were about a campaign, yet they may not be able to pinpoint the contributions of particular media sources to that knowledge base. If this is the case, and if Cleveland's newspapers provided a great deal of coverage concerning the congressional campaigns, then the well-informed House voter in Cleveland may overestimate the amount of information received from broadcast media. Conversely, poorly informed Pittsburgh voters know that they received little information from *any* source, and thus they report receiving little information from broadcast media.

Second, and more simply, print coverage may drive broadcast coverage at the local level. Television and radio news directors may disagree,

TABLE 3.10. Amount of Information Received from Broadcast Media and Local Newspapers about the 1992 U.S. House Campaigns

	Broadcast Media		Local Newspapers	
	Cuyahoga County	Allegheny County	Cuyahoga County	Allegheny County
A great deal	109 (40.0)	99 (31.3)	109 (40.0)	21 (6.6)
Some	138 (45.5)	124 (39.2)	135 (44.6)	59 (18.6)
Only a little	47 (15.5)	73 (23.1)	42 (13.9)	99 (31.2)
None at all	9 (3.0)	20 (6.3)	17 (5.6)	138 (43.5)
Mean	2.145	1.956	2.109	0.883
N	303	316	303	317
t-value, Cuyahoga vs. Allegheny	2.801		17.096	

Note: Percentages are in parentheses. Means and t-values are calculated with data coded 3 = a great deal, to 0 = none at all.

but campaign managers claim that the best way to get their candidates mentioned on the evening's broadcast news reports is to first get their candidates mentioned in the morning paper. That is, local broadcast news organizations may look to newspapers for some of their stories (McManus 1990). In a personal interview, a spokesperson for one of the Cleveland congressional candidates explains:

> Newspapers in many ways set the agenda and set the tone. Many TV and radio newscasters will key their stories off of what's in the morning newspaper.

In Pittsburgh, this phenomenon presumably would have caused local television and radio stations responding to the newspaper strike either to adapt their methods of reporting on the congressional campaigns or to decrease the quantity of that coverage. Interviews with representatives of Pittsburgh's congressional candidates provide evidence for the latter. For example, one spokesperson explained that

> The spin-off to local TV and radio wasn't the same this year. They generate much of their coverage from what's in the *Post-Gazette* in the morning. They didn't adapt (to the newspaper strike) effectively, at least in terms of coverage of the congressional elections.

From this perspective, the newspaper strike possibly hurt the entire structure of local news reporting, and thus diminished the quality of broadcast coverage of the local House campaigns.

It is likely that Pittsburgh voters reported receiving comparatively little information from broadcast media due to a combination of the two factors described here. However, regardless of the reason, it is still the case that this information gap appears only for the House races. Hence, we can safely conclude that Pittsburgh residents received less campaign information about the House elections, regardless of source, than did Cleveland residents. In contrast, such a conclusion is not supported for the Senate or presidential elections. Pittsburgh voters' increased reliance on broadcast media may have partially offset the information dearth for the Senate and presidential campaigns. Additionally, Pittsburgh voters relied significantly on national print media for news about the Senate and presidential contests, and information from those sources also may have helped to close the information gap caused by the newspaper strike.

What can we conclude from analysis of the amount of information voters received from local newspapers and broadcast media? First, it is now clear that one essential methodological hurdle has been crossed. The strike caused a substantial reduction in the quantity of information voters received from local newspapers concerning the 1992 presidential, Senate, and U.S. House elections. Therefore, at minimum, subsequent quasi-experimental tests will be able to determine if local newspapers play a unique electoral role. Second, and more substantively, voters perceive themselves as being relatively well informed about national-level political campaigns. Overall, over 70 percent of respondents report receiving either some or a great deal of information about each of the three campaigns. Third, voters' perceptions regarding the amount of campaign information they have received vary greatly by electoral contest. More specifically, voters view themselves as having been much more fully informed about the presidential election than about the corresponding Senate or U.S. House races. Fourth, we again see that the relative importance of local newspapers increases for lower-level offices. In Cleveland, voters report receiving as much information about the U.S. House races from newspapers as from broadcast media, even though respondents were more likely to list broadcast media as their top source for campaign news.

Tuning Out?

Data regarding the quantity of information received by voters clearly indicate that most individuals prefer to obtain at least some news about the candidates for national office. Hence, it appears that voters are not casting their ballots haphazardly. However, voters are content with varying amounts of information for different elections, and the willingness of voters to acquire campaign news seemingly hinges to some extent on the ease with which those reports can be obtained. Importantly, the costs of information acquisition vary for different news sources. For example, the flurry of televised news concerning the 1992 presidential campaign provided voters with extremely efficient access to electoral information. Conversely, news about congressional elections generally is much more scarce, meaning that the voter must engage in a comparatively active search in order to develop an information base comparable to the one so readily available for the presidential campaign.

Thus far, evidence has been mixed regarding the willingness of voters to put forth effort in obtaining campaign news. On the positive side, many voters prefer print over broadcast media despite the required expenditure of greater cognitive effort. Further, faced with an extended newspaper strike, many voters in Pittsburgh apparently endeavored to replace print with print, again demonstrating a willingness on the part of the electorate to assume a relatively active role in the process of information acquisition. However, on the negative side, the amount of information received by voters declines for lower-level races, indicating that ease of access may be a critical determinant of information acquisition. Also, the effort expended by Pittsburgh-area voters in searching for alternative print media seems limited; many voters simply joined the procession on the road most traveled—television.

It seems fair to state that voters have their limits. That is, voters willingly pay a price to acquire news about political campaigns, yet many individuals seem likely to balk if the price is too high. If we can identify these limits, then insight can be gained regarding the types of campaign strategies that will maximize the depth of the voter's information base. A critical question is whether the voter's attentiveness to the news varies as a function of access to information. In short, can we spark effort on the part of the voter by increasing the availability of campaign news?

In addition to questions concerning media-use patterns and the quantity of information received from various news sources, Cleveland and Pittsburgh respondents were asked how much attention they paid to news about the presidential, Senate, and House campaigns. We have seen that voters in Pittsburgh usually found substitutes for their missing newspapers. However, when forced toward these alternatives, did the willingness of voters to acquire campaign news suffer? If so, if some voters "tuned out," this would suggest that campaign coverage contributes to an informed electorate both by providing the actual news material and by activating a willingness among voters to attend to those campaign reports.

Analysis of attentiveness data serves a second function. The postelection survey does not include items measuring the total amount of information voters received about the presidential, Senate, and House elections. However, a general indicator of information acquisition is needed so that we may determine if Pittsburgh's newspaper strike reduced only the amount of information voters received from local newspapers, or if it limited media exposure more broadly. The attentiveness items provide the necessary data. Evidence that Pittsburgh's strike caused voters to become less attentive to campaign news would suggest that the strike affected general levels of media exposure rather than just exposure to local newspapers.

The self-reported attentiveness of Cleveland and Pittsburgh voters is depicted in table 3.11. Approximately two-thirds of voters claim to have paid a great deal of attention to news about the presidential race, but only half that many voters paid comparable attention to the Ohio and Pennsylvania Senate contests. In Cleveland, this decline does not continue with the House campaigns; instead, similar attentiveness scores are reported for the Senate and House elections. However, voters in the Pittsburgh area admit to being relatively inattentive to news concerning the congressional elections.

The absence of access to a major local newspaper did not cause voters to shrug off news about the presidential or Senate races. Cleveland and Pittsburgh results are virtually identical for the presidential and Senate elections, confirming that attentiveness to campaign news about these races was in no way harmed by the lack of a major local newspaper. Rather than tuning out, would-be newspaper readers simply turned to alternative media. In particular, we have seen that magazines and national newspapers played a prominent role in the presidential race, as did television in the Pennsylvania Senate race. With viable substitutes readily available, voters displayed a level of flexibility sufficient to preserve the process of information acquisition.

In contrast with these results, the strike produced a substantial decline in attentiveness to news about the House campaigns. Hence, the tangible effect of the strike on information acquisition is that many

TABLE 3.11. Attentiveness to Campaign News

	Presidential		Senate		House	
	Cuyahoga County	Allegheny County	Cuyahoga County	Allegheny County	Cuyahoga County	Allegheny County
A great deal	203 (65.9)	217 (66.6)	95 (31.0)	116 (36.1)	100 (33.0)	65 (20.5)
Some	85 (27.6)	88 (27.0)	155 (50.7)	134 (41.7)	139 (45.9)	121 (38.2)
Only a little	20 (6.5)	19 (5.8)	49 (16.0)	64 (19.9)	54 (17.8)	114 (36.0)
None at all	0 (0)	2 (.6)	7 (2.3)	7 (2.2)	10 (3.3)	17 (5.4)
Mean	2.594	2.595	2.105	2.118	2.086	1.738
N	308	326	306	321	303	317
t-value, Cuyahoga vs. Allegheny	-0.019		-0.224		5.267	

Note: Percentages are in parentheses. Means and *t*-values are calculated with data coded 3 = a great deal, to 0 = none at all.

Pittsburgh-area voters limited their attentiveness to news concerning their respective congressional elections. Why did voters tune out only for the House campaign? The most plausible explanation centers on the cost of substitute news sources. Whereas voters could remain attentive to news about the presidential and Senate races without expending much more time or effort than that required to read the local newspaper, replacement costs were greater for the congressional elections. A comparatively active search was required for the voter to remain informed about the House contests, and many voters apparently declined to expend such effort. To a degree, attentiveness hinges on the availability of information. Hence, it appears that media may contribute to an informed electorate not only by providing information, but also by sparking voter interest in political campaigns.

In table 3.1, we saw three possible scenarios regarding the impact of Pittsburgh's newspaper strike on media exposure. The first scenario, that the strike had no effect on media exposure, can be ruled out. Voters changed their media-use patterns in response to the strike, an alteration necessitated by the fact that the strike reduced the amount of information voters received from local newspapers about the presidential, Senate, and House campaigns. At question is whether the strike limited only exposure to information from local newspapers (scenario two), or media exposure more generally (scenario three). If the strike did not affect overall levels of media exposure, then quasi-experimental tests can examine the possibility that newspapers are uniquely important sources of electoral news. Alternatively, if the strike did limit media exposure, then quasi-experimental tests can examine general media effects.

The strike did not reduce overall levels of media exposure for the presidential or Senate campaigns. Voters' attentiveness to news about these campaigns was unaffected by the absence of newspapers. The combination of easy access to relevant broadcast news and the availability of national print media provided ample information to fill the gap caused by the lack of access to local newspapers. The strike limited access to newspapers but did not affect general levels of media exposure. Therefore, quasi-experimental tests using data for the Senate and presidential elections will determine if the local newspaper has a different effect than other media sources on voters' knowledge levels, the dynamics of interpersonal political discussion, and electoral choice. For the Senate and presidential elections, Cleveland versus Pittsburgh tests will pit the newspaper-rich versus the newspaper-poor.

Quasi-experimental tests will evaluate general media effects when data concern this study's six U.S. House elections. General media effects can be examined because the newspaper strike reduced overall levels of media exposure for the House campaigns. In response to the strike, Pittsburgh voters became inattentive to news about the local House races. Not only were levels of information received from local newspapers affected, but Pittsburgh voters also report receiving low levels of information about the House campaigns from broadcast media compared with their Cleveland counterparts. Many Pittsburgh voters failed even to name two sources of news about the 1992 House elections. Thus, for the House campaigns, Cleveland versus Pittsburgh tests offer a comparison of the media-rich versus the media-poor.

By luck rather than by design, Pittsburgh's newspaper strike has created an optimal research context. The strike lasted throughout the entire 1992 general election season, providing a quasi-experimental manipulation infinitely more pervasive than a laboratory experiment could offer. Further, because the strike influenced media exposure in a different manner for the House campaigns than for the Senate and presidential elections, the quasi-experimental tests to be conducted in the following chapters can provide new perspectives regarding both the specific significance of local newspapers and the general importance of news media for information acquisition in U.S. elections.

Conclusion

This chapter provides context. Now that the manipulation checks have been passed, the Cleveland-Pittsburgh data will enable attention to numerous specific questions regarding the electoral significance of local newspapers. However, although this has been a chapter of manipulation checks, the results also provide important evidence regarding voters' patterns of media exposure. Further, the ability of Pittsburgh voters to locate alternative media sources speaks to the quality of electoral behavior.

In examining media-use patterns, we may ask a simple empirical question: do newspapers matter? Although the question is simple, the answer is multifaceted. First, data from the Cleveland and Pittsburgh samples indicate that television rather than the local newspaper is the dominant source of electoral news. Thus, newspapers are not of preeminent importance as news sources for national elections. However, a second clear finding is that local newspapers are the only media source to rival television in the electoral arena. Among Cleveland-area voters, a strong majority listed the local newspaper as one of the top two sources of news for the presidential, Senate, and House campaigns. Third, the importance of local newspapers varies as a function of both individual and contextual forces. More specifically, we have seen that the likelihood of reliance on newspapers rather than television increases across civics knowledge, and increases for lower-level political campaigns. Finally, it appears that the information value of local newspapers may be greater than the information value of broadcast media. In the House elections, for example, Cleveland voters reported television to be their primary news source, yet those same voters claimed to have received equivalent amounts of information about the House campaigns from broadcast media and local newspapers.

Several aspects of this chapter's results suggest that extensive criticism of voters' information acquisition is unwarranted. First, media use is adapted on an election-specific basis. Exposure to news about Senate and House contests is not merely a by-product of attentiveness to the presidential campaign. Instead, many voters turn to different media sources for the three elections in an apparent attempt to tailor the information search to match the realities of media coverage. Second, voters willingly expend some amount of effort in acquiring campaign information. The electorate is not a passive news audience. For example, many voters in the Pittsburgh area turned to national print media for news about the presidential campaign. The easy, or passive, strategy would be for the voter to rely on broadcast rather than print media in all cases. More importantly, voters lacking access to a major local newspaper presumably should find it much easier to fall back on broadcast media than to locate alternative print sources. Hence, the manner in which Pittsburgh voters adapted to the newspaper strike demonstrates some willingness on the part of voters to *participate* in the process of learning about candidates.

Despite this note of optimism, we must be careful not to overestimate the quality of information acquisition. First, some Pittsburgh voters who shifted to national print sources may be exhibiting a general preference to read, more than a specific quest for news concerning political campaigns. Second, the evidence is clear that both the amount of information received from news media and voters' self-reported attentiveness to the news declines for lower-level races. When bombarded with news concerning the presidential election, voters attend to that news. However, news consumption falls with considerable speed for Senate and House campaigns. Finally, Pittsburgh data arguably indicate that when the going gets tough, many voters simply give up. Information acquisition was surely the most difficult for the U.S. House races within Allegheny County. How did voters respond? A sizable portion failed even to name two sources of news for the House elections, and the self-reported attentiveness to news concerning these contests was minimal. Voters desire some level of news about candidates, and voters will expend some level of effort to obtain that news. However, voters also have their limits, and thus many will accept a weak information base rather than engaging in particularly burdensome information searches.

CHAPTER 4

Newspapers and Political Knowledge

I couldn't quite recall the name
But the pose looked familiar to me
    —Bruce Springsteen

Many of the most significant questions facing researchers interested in the relationship between news media and electoral behavior concern the extent to which media facilitate learning about politics. Do voters learn anything from media? If so, what do they learn—information about issues, or information about which candidate is ahead in the polls? Are some media sources particularly well suited to convey news about political affairs, or do all media possess some capacity to inform their audiences? Can journalistic practices be changed to help citizens better understand politics?

Such questions are important on a normative level. Effective democratic governance presupposes the existence of an informed citizenry. Popular input into government will be vacuous if citizens do not understand how the political system operates, or if citizens fail to comprehend the intricacies of contemporary policy debates. Consequently, many analysts have been disturbed by evidence that Americans as a whole possess what appears to be a very weak understanding of politics (for reviews, see Kinder 1983; Kinder and Sears 1985; Neuman 1986). For example, Stephen Bennett (1988) presents a scathing critique of citizenship in the United States, drawing on evidence that a large portion of Americans cannot pass a test of basic political knowledge. Much of the statistical evidence has become part of the common lore of American politics. For instance, we know that barely half of the persons surveyed as part of the National Election Studies are able to name the congressional candidates in their district (Yeric and Todd 1989), and that knowledge levels are substantially lower for questions concerning specific policies and issues (e.g., Kuklinski, Metlay, and Kay 1982; Sigelman and Yanarella 1986).

The precise implication of such low levels of knowledge has been the center of much debate. Elsewhere, I have argued that low levels of textbook knowledge are insufficient to establish that individuals fail as capable political participants. The value of textbook knowledge should not be exaggerated, because the widespread use of reliable simplifying mechanisms minimizes the amount of information people need to construct meaningful political judgments (e.g., Mondak 1993c, 1993d, 1994). Others have advanced similar claims, including Popkin (1991), and Sniderman and his colleagues (Sniderman, Brody, and Tetlock 1991). A related perspective is offered by Page and Shapiro (1992), who suggest that aggregate public opinion, the input in a political system, can be rational even if large portions of the citizenry lack a detailed understanding of political affairs.

My intention in this chapter is not to debate all aspects of the knowledge issue, but rather to examine the relationship between news media and political awareness. Television is one of the alleged culprits responsible for low levels of political knowledge in the United States. Newspapers, the argument goes, are relatively well suited to convey information about politics, but the growing significance of television has numbed the minds of the American citizenry. This line of reasoning raises the central empirical question to be addressed in this chapter: do local newspapers uniquely contribute to the information base of the American electorate? Previous research on this question has produced conflicting evidence, in part because of the variety of methodological approaches that analysts have employed. Following a brief review of this research, we will consider what can be learned by examining the impact of Pittsburgh's newspaper strike on levels of political awareness.

Broadcast Media, Print Media, and Information Acquisition

Considerable scholarly attention has been devoted to assessment of what viewers learn from television (e.g., Robinson and Levy 1986; Gunter 1987), and, more specifically, what role television plays in producing an informed electorate (e.g., Patterson and McClure 1976; Patterson 1980). In contrast, relatively few studies directly examine the capacity of local newspapers to facilitate political learning. Further, no consensus has emerged from those studies that have specifically investigated the information value of local newspapers.

Cross-sectional individual-level studies typically have produced evidence suggesting that citizens learn more from newspapers than from television. In these studies, survey data provide a measure of the respondents' levels of political awareness, and also indicate each respondent's primary news source. Regressing the former variable on the latter usually demonstrates that people who turn to newspapers as their primary source of news know more than people who turn to broadcast media (e.g., Robinson and Levy 1986; Robinson and Davis 1990; Berkowtiz and Pritchard 1989; Weaver and Drew 1993). Consider a central conclusion offered by Robinson and Levy (1986, 233), following their extensive review of the media-effects literature:

> Heavier exposure to print media is generally associated with higher levels of news comprehension. . . . [N]ewspaper readers, and to a lesser extent magazine readers, were consistently found to be more informed than nonreaders. Print media use is not merely a surrogate variable for education, given that these differences held up after control for education and other predictors.

Such a conclusion is reasonable if offered as a statement of correlation. That is, for whatever reason, those people who read newspapers the most tend to know more about current events than those people who read newspapers the least. However, Robinson and Levy suggest that they have identified a causal relationship; it is in part *because* they read newspapers that some people know more than others. Unfortunately, such a conclusion is highly suspect. The number of factors distinguishing newspaper readers and nonreaders may well be limitless, and any combination of those factors may account for the differential knowledge levels so frequently cited in cross-sectional studies. In a stunning case of methodological oversight, many early cross-sectional studies failed to include statistical controls for any characteristics of the survey respondents, yet still boldly claimed that exposure to print media is a causal determinant of information acquisition (see Robinson and Levy 1986 for a review).

More recently, as the quote from Robinson and Levy suggests, investigators have included controls for education, interest, and so on, in their statistical models. However, the task of identifying causal relationships is not so simple that it can be accomplished merely by introducing a few control variables. First, no study can account for all possible determinants of information acquisition. If any potential control variable is not included in a statistical model, then the relationship between exposure to print media and news comprehension still may be spurious. Second, and more fundamentally, because the control variables are correlated with the choice of a primary news medium, it is not possible to derive a unique statistical estimate for any of the independent variables.[1]

Regardless of these methodological limitations, the conclusion that exposure to newspapers promotes learning has gained wide acceptance in both media studies and political science. In particular, many analysts voice acceptance of the claim that print media best facilitate the acquisition of factual information (e.g., Graber 1993; Davis 1992; Owen 1991). One textbook on media and politics states the point bluntly: "Newspapers contribute more to issue awareness than television; television news viewing has little effect on issue learning" (Davis 1992, 245). Although the evidence supporting such a conclusion remains weak, this perspective does hold considerable intuitive appeal. It is true, after all, that newspapers possess greater capacity than broadcast media to provide extensive coverage of a story. If print media can deliver more detail, then they may well outperform broadcast media in promoting learning about issues.

In contrast with this view, several recent studies cast substantial doubt on the claim that newspapers hold some unique ability to foster information acquisition. Graber (1990) integrates a content analysis of televised news stories with an experimental design, and finds that television's visual images promote information gain. Such a conclusion undercuts the thesis that print media possess a universal advantage over their broadcast counterparts. Graber advances what I view to be a very reasonable argument by noting that television and print each have strengths and weaknesses as information sources; blanket comparisons of print and broadcast media miss the point that each medium may excel in reporting particular types of news stories.

Price and Zaller (1993) offer compelling evidence that newspaper exposure does not uniquely heighten news reception. It is Price and Zaller's thesis that existing political knowledge better predicts who gets the news than conventional indicators of media exposure, interest, and education. Their study of reception of 16 news stories demonstrates that an individual's general knowledge about politics strongly affects the likelihood that that individual will receive information about subsequent news stories. More important for current purposes is Price and Zaller's finding that newspaper exposure generally is not related to news recall in multivariate statistical models that account for the influence of prior political knowledge.

Using a multimethod approach, Neuman, Just, and Crigler (1992) present findings similar to those of the Price and Zaller study (see also Just and Crigler 1989). Specifically, Neuman and his colleagues show that the relationship between knowledge and news medium evaporates when statistical controls capture the influence of variance in the cognitive skill of their study's participants. Prior political knowledge and cognitive skill, two very different variables, both do damage to the purported impact of newspaper exposure on information acquisition. The reason these variables act similarly is that both serve to indicate the individual's motivation and ability to assimilate new information. The acquisition of new information comes most easily for persons generally familiar with the issue in question, and for persons willing to expend the effort needed to process the new data. Some people want to get the news, and some do not. Once analysts account for prior knowledge or cognitive skill, it appears that learning from the news occurs just as easily from television as from local newspapers. Education, the most fashionable control variable in many cross-sectional studies, is a poor substitute for the knowledge and skill variables tested by Price and Zaller (1993) and Neuman, Just, and Crigler (1992).

Although Neuman, Just, and Crigler draw on several methodologies, their critical results emerge from laboratory experiments. One of the most interesting findings is that television coverage not only successfully conveyed factual information to the study's participants, but also produced higher levels of learning than did newspapers. This result establishes that broadcast media *can* match or surpass print media in the ability to foster information acquisition. Nevertheless, the reality of learning outside of the laboratory still may be very different. The laboratory context is far more pristine than the real world. It may be that television's theoretical capabilities are rarely met in reality, where ringing telephones, barking dogs, and burning dinners provide distractions that laboratory participants simply do not face. Likewise, Price and Zaller's political knowledge variable possibly reflects the accumulated benefits of long-term exposure to newspapers, in which case they may underestimate the effects of newspapers on political learning.

When different methods produce different results, interpretation largely hinges on one's assessment of the competing research designs. Due to their relative methodological sophistication, I am more persuaded by the Price and Zaller (1993) and Neuman, Just, and Crigler (1992) studies than by the various cross-sectional investigations that trumpet the superiority of print media. Still, more definitive evidence would emerge if we could compare the knowledge levels of individuals who live in a world with newspapers with those of individuals who do not have access to newspapers. Such comparison, of course, is the objective of this chapter.

Prior to examining evidence from the postelection survey, it is worth noting that dispute regarding the significance of newspapers in fostering understanding of issues extends beyond academic circles. Specifically, postelection interviews with representatives of the candidates in this study's elections produced conflicting views on the question of whether local newspapers are more adept than broadcast media at providing issue coverage.[2] Several of the persons I interviewed voiced the opinion that newspapers do report on issues in greater depth than do broadcast media:

Without the strike, there would have been more information about where the candidates stood on the issues.

More substance can be gained from a newspaper than from broadcast media. Broadcast media are more superficial.

The *Press* and the *Post-Gazette* pick up on issues. Change for the sake of change would not have gotten a lot of attention.

Without newspapers, we could not draw differences between his position and our position.

Clearly, you get more information out through print.

With TV, you reach many more people. The benefit of newspapers is the ability to go in-depth more so than on TV. We did not see quite as much depth on TV as in the papers. When dealing with issues that are a little more complex, the benefits of print media are there.

It is perhaps noteworthy that the first four of these six statements were offered by persons associated with campaigns in the Pittsburgh area. With the local newspapers absent, the campaign organizations apparently perceived there to be a dearth of issue coverage. Only one Pittsburgh interview yielded any element of dissent from this view:

With papers, there would have been no difference at all on the issues; the issues themselves would not have changed.

Praise for the issue reporting in local newspapers was not so universal in Cleveland. Two Cleveland interviews produced particularly stinging criticism of the *Plain Dealer*'s campaign coverage:

The type of coverage absolutely affected what the voters knew. In a perfect world, the papers would have stuck to the issues. Instead, they tried to draw us into mudslinging. The way we could have gotten press was by attacking our opponent.

Newspapers have more of an obligation to go into greater detail on issues, to deemphasize the sound-bite mentality. They did not succeed. The *Plain Dealer* expanded upon television advertisements. They focused far too much on polling and polling data. Newspapers chimed in, and went with the less substantive parts of the campaign.

Note that in both of these statements there exists an implicit recognition that newspapers have the *potential* to cover issues more thoroughly than can broadcast media. These individuals do not doubt the theoretical capability of print media to inform voters. The second statement is especially interesting on this point, with its reference to an obligation on the part of newspapers to focus on issues. The objection in both cases centers not on what newspapers *can* accomplish, but instead on what they actually *did* accomplish in reporting the 1992 campaigns.

Plaudits for newspapers flowed most freely in the Pittsburgh interviews, perhaps proving only that absence makes the heart grow fonder. Ultimately, doubt remains as to whether local newspapers possess a unique ability to inform the electorate. Previous studies have generated conflicting evidence, and interviews with campaign officials have produced conflicting opinions. Fortunately, the Pittsburgh newspaper strike allows a new perspective. In the following sections, two distinct measures of political knowledge are analyzed. For both, quasi-experimental comparison of Pittsburgh and Cleveland data aids in the effort to determine the impact of local newspapers on information acquisition.

Subjective Measures of Knowledge

To determine the impact of local newspapers on political knowledge, knowledge scores for Cleveland and Pittsburgh respondents are compared. But how should knowledge be measured? The most commonly used technique is the objective test; survey respondents answer a "quiz" designed to measure political awareness. However, considerable caution must be exercised to construct an effective objective measure of political knowledge (see Delli Carpini and Keeter 1993). Further, analysis of how well survey respondents recall a few stray facts about politics arguably sidetracks us from study of the fundamental dynamics of political behavior. Neuman, Just, and Crigler (1992) suggest, for instance, that researchers should examine what citizens *do* know rather than dwelling on interpretation of characteristically low scores on objective knowledge measures. Teachers recognize that the student who best remembers names and dates does not necessarily hold the best understanding of history. Likewise, the voter who can recall the names of every candidate for every office may not possess a particularly deep understanding of political affairs.

In this study, the objective measure of political knowledge brings an especially pragmatic limitation. Because survey respondents faced two distinct sets of Senate candidates and six sets of House candidates, the utility of objective questions concerning those elections would be highly suspect. For instance, recognition of candidates' names presumably would be affected more by how long the incumbents had served than by access to a local newspaper. Similarly, no single measure focusing on campaign issues could be constructed because the importance of particular issues varies from one House or Senate race to another.

Despite possible limitations, the objective measure of political knowledge may be our best tool to identify voters' levels of political awareness. Hence, an extensive battery of knowledge items was included on the postelection survey, and the results are analyzed in the next section. Still, such questions alone do not provide a fully satisfactory indicator of political knowledge. As a complement to objective recall items, the postelection survey also included a very simple alternative: respondents were asked to assess how much they themselves knew about the 1992 presidential, Senate, and U.S. House candidates.

What are the strengths and weaknesses of such subjective measures? On the plus side, each question's parameters match perfectly the domain of interest. For example, rather than sampling a respondent's recall of various facts concerning a U.S. House race, a single item can be used to capture the entirety of the subject. The down side, of course, involves the highly subjective nature of self-assessment. The ability to recall the candidates' names may constitute a high level of knowledge for one respondent, whereas a second respondent might be disappointed if unable to remember the candidates' positions on a wide array of specific policies. However, this limitation does not hamper comparison of Cleveland and Pittsburgh data. What is "some" knowledge to one respondent may be "a great deal" of knowledge to another, but there is no reason to believe that what is "some" knowledge in Cleveland constitutes "a great deal" of knowledge in Pittsburgh. In other words, aggregate statistics drawn from respondents' self-reports can enable meaningful comparison of regional effects even if the underlying individual-level data have apparent limitations.

Table 4.1 displays results for the self-reported measures of political knowledge. The data instill at least some confidence that respondents' self-reports provide useful information. First, respondents willingly admitted to being imperfectly informed. Some respondents may have exaggerated their knowledge levels, but the aggregate scores fall far enough below the theoretical maximum of 3.0 to suggest that such exaggeration was not universal. Second, results form an intuitively appealing pattern, with self-reported knowledge reaching its highest point for the presidential race, and its lowest for the U.S. House elections. It is highly plausible that respondents as a whole were indeed considerably more informed about the presidential candidates than about the Senate candidates, and were somewhat more informed about the Senate candidates than about the House candidates. In short, the distribution of results suggests that the self-report items do provide valid and meaningful indicators of political awareness.

Comparing results for Cleveland and Pittsburgh, we see very different patterns for the three sets of elections. At the presidential level, scores reach high marks in both Cleveland and Pittsburgh. The advantage in Pittsburgh is substantively minor, but the effect does achieve statistical significance. Together, results for the presidential and Senate elections are most revealing when considered from the perspective of Pittsburgh's newspaper strike: voters without access to a major local newspaper perceived themselves to be at least as well informed about the 1992 presidential and Senate elections as voters who did have access to a local newspaper. In chapter 3, we saw that the strike did not limit media exposure for the Senate and presidential races, due to the availability of alternative news sources. Table 4.1 demonstrates the substantive implication of that finding; access to local newspapers does not uniquely enhance voters' perceptions of their own knowledge levels when access to alternative media sources is not constrained.

In contrast with results for the presidential and Senate elections, scores for the House races suggest that media exposure does influence political knowledge. Self-perceived knowledge is a full quarter of a point lower in Pittsburgh than in Cleveland, and the effect reaches the highest level of statistical significance. The analysis in chapter 3 demonstrated that Pittsburgh voters were not able to find fully satisfactory alternatives to the striking newspapers for news about the local U.S. House races. Table 4.1 reveals that living in a media-poor decision-making context brings an important tangible implication: when media

TABLE 4.1. Self-Reported Knowledge about the 1992 Presidential, Senate, and U.S. House Campaigns

	Cuyahoga County	Allegheny County	t-value	N
Presidential	2.537	2.666	-2.624*	631
Senate	1.997	2.065	-0.068	635
House	1.967	1.717	3.702**	630

Note: Cell entries are regional means. Data are drawn from three questions: "By the end of the campaign, how much did you know about this year's presidential/ Senate/ congressional candidates—a great deal, some, only a little, or none at all?" Results are coded 0 (none at all) to 3 (a great deal).
 * $p < .01$, ** $p < .001$

exposure is limited, voters report a corresponding decline in their knowledge about the subject in question.

For years, analysts have engaged in heated debate regarding the relative worth of print and broadcast media as information sources. New perspective is gained by stepping back and considering what the audience members themselves have to say about the question. Self-reported knowledge levels reveal that voters perceive that lack of access to a major local newspaper brings no handicap whatsoever provided that alternative news sources are available. Pittsburgh's presidential and Senate voters were entirely unfazed by the absence of their daily newspapers. If self-reported measures of knowledge can be accepted as valid, then these results indicate that local newspapers enjoy no unique ability to enhance the information base of the electorate. Only for the House races, where the newspaper strike limited actual media exposure, did Pittsburgh voters perceive that their knowledge about the candidates suffered.

Objective Measures of Knowledge

Measures of political knowledge based on survey respondents' own perceptions are useful because the questions can be designed to capture very specific knowledge domains. Still, the validity of such measures can be debated. Much like an academic course in which students grade their own performance, self-reported measures of political knowledge are hampered by the varying predispositions and whims of a survey's respondents. What is only a little knowledge to one respondent may be a great deal to another. In this study, self-reported knowledge levels provide important data. Nevertheless, additional measures are needed if we are to assess more precisely how access to a local newspaper affects information acquisition.

Rather than relying on self-reports, most studies of political knowledge draw on batteries of objective items. In essence, the survey respondent answers a quiz designed to measure political awareness. This approach overcomes the subjectivity of self-reports, but objective measures must be administered and interpreted with caution. First, the survey respondent may become uncomfortable or embarrassed when asked to answer an extended series of questions concerning political affairs. This risk must be minimized, because the survey interview must not be an unpleasant experience for those persons who graciously take the time to participate in our studies. Second, I believe that it is highly presumptuous of the investigator to dictate what respondents *should* know about politics. Carefully designed objective knowledge measures can help us to differentiate levels of knowledge within the electorate, but it is simply wrong to use results to conclude that some percentage of voters fail to meet a highly arbitrary standard of political awareness.

One additional point warrants brief attention. This chapter's objective knowledge measures focus on national and international affairs. However, perhaps it is the case that most people do not read the local newspaper to acquire such news. People who turn to print media for national and international news may have as their primary source either magazines or national newspapers. If this is the case, then the deck would be stacked against the print superiority thesis by virtue of this study's design. However, for most people the local newspaper clearly is the primary print medium for national and international news. First, local newspapers win the battle versus magazines and national papers largely by default; the combined weekly circulation of the top magazines is under ten million, and the combined daily circulation of the top national newspapers is barely five million (Davis 1992). Second, local papers do cover national and international affairs. In October, 1992, for example, there were 218 front-page stories in the Cleveland *Plain Dealer*. Of these, 68 percent concerned national or international events. Third, surveys show that national print sources have little reach compared with the local newspaper. We saw in chapter 3, for instance, that 19.4 percent of Cleveland respondents said that the local newspaper was their primary source of news about the 1992 presidential campaign, and 46.9 percent said it was their second source. The comparable scores for national newspapers and magazines combined are only 5.8 percent and 9.1 percent.

The postelection survey includes 17 questions designed to measure respondents' knowledge of national and international affairs. Again, my objective is quite simple: to determine if access to a major local newspaper affects levels of political awareness. Hence, rather than constructing some artificial knowledge threshold, the analysis will center on relative effects; do respondents in Cleveland know more (or less) than respondents in Pittsburgh about topics that were in the national news during the time of Pittsburgh's newspaper strike? Table 4.2 displays the wording of the knowledge questions, and reports results for Cleveland and Pittsburgh respondents. The results will be examined in detail momentarily. For now, it is sufficient to note that differences between Cleveland and Pittsburgh are minimal. In no case does the gap reach conventional levels of statistical significance, and only three items (2, 3, and 17) even approach statistical significance.

The 17 items form three distinct batteries. First, questions 1–5 focus on matters that were in the news contemporaneous with the 1992 campaigns, but that did not directly concern the campaigns. These current events items were constructed using a two-step procedure. First, the news

TABLE 4.2. Objective Measures of Political Knowledge

Question	Coding	Percentage of Respondents Answering Correctly		t-value
		Cuyahoga County	Allegheny County	
1. About how large was the federal budget deficit for fiscal year 1992?	1 if between $200 and $400 billion; 0 if otherwise	11.7	13.2	-0.571
2. More than 500 people died in an earthquake in mid-October. Where was that earthquake?	1 if Egypt, Africa, or the Middle East; 0 if otherwise	10.7	6.5	1.896*
3. What is NAFTA?	1 if the North American Free Trade Agreement, or any mention of trade; 0 if otherwise	12.0	8.0	1.675*
4. Since coming to office in 1989, President Bush has vetoed over 40 bills. How many of these vetoes have been overridden by Congress?	1 if one; 0 if otherwise	26.6	25.5	0.311
5. On what continent is the nation of Somalia located?	1 if Africa; 0 if otherwise	59.4	57.2	0.557
6. Immediately after Ross Perot officially entered the presidential race in early October, what was his standing in the polls? (about what percentage of registered voters said they planned to vote for Perot at that time?)	1 if between 5% and 10%; 0 if otherwise	32.9	29.2	0.996
7. As a result of this year's elections, which party will have the most members in the U.S. House of Representatives in Washington?	1 if Democratic; 0 if otherwise	86.7	84.9	0.651

TABLE 4.2. — *Continued*

8. Which state has the most electoral college votes?	1 if California; 0 if otherwise	66.6	63.7	0.756
9. About how many Democratic and Republican candidates for senator this year were women?	1 if ten, eleven, or twelve; 0 if otherwise	11.4	14.5	-1.158
10. According to public opinion polls, which candidate won the first presidential debate?	1 if Clinton or Perot; 0 if otherwise	82.5	80.3	0.697
11. There were three formats for this year's presidential debates: a panel of journalists, questions from an audience, and a single moderator. Which of these was the format recommended by the bipartisan presidential commission on debates?	1 if single moderator; 0 if otherwise	22.4	27.4	-1.446
12. For each of the following issues, please tell me which candidate—George Bush, Bill Clinton, or Ross Perot—took the position I describe. First, which candidate proposed that retired federal government employees have their cost of living increases reduced by one-third over the next five years?	1 if Perot; 0 if otherwise	35.5	33.5	0.548
13. Which candidate proposed a 50-cents per gallon gasoline tax, to be phased in over five years?	1 if Perot; 0 if otherwise	65.6	66.3	-0.179
14. Which candidate proposed reducing U.S. troop strength in Europe to approximately 150,000?	1 if Bush; 0 if otherwise	13.6	15.3	-0.607

TABLE 4.2. — *Continued*

15. Which candidate supported motor-voter legislation that allows citizens to register to vote when getting their drivers' licenses?	1 if Clinton; 0 if otherwise	38.0	37.1	0.226
16. Which candidate supported statehood for the District of Columbia?	1 if Clinton; 0 if otherwise	34.4	34.7	-0.065
17. Which candidate supported amending the Constitution to require a balanced federal budget?	1 if Bush; 0 if otherwise	26.9	20.6	1.889*

* $p < .10$

sections of all September and October, 1992, issues of the Cleveland *Plain Dealer* were analyzed to select topics for possible inclusion on the postelection survey. Second, approximately 80 students in two political science courses at the University of Pittsburgh answered an extensive series of knowledge items resulting from that analysis. In choosing which items to include on the public opinion survey, I first selected questions that had been answered correctly by at least 20 percent of students on the pretest. Among the resulting subset, I then picked five questions that varied in degree of difficulty. Zaller (1992) argues that when only a few items are used to measure a knowledge domain, it is best that a mix of easy and difficult questions be included. This approach reduces the average interitem correlation, but facilitates construction of a scale that better differentiates knowledge levels than if all questions are of midlevel difficulty (see also Delli Carpini and Keeter 1993).

In table 4.2, results for the first five items reveal that the questions did indeed vary in difficulty. The consistently low scores for questions 1–3 are unfortunate, but the battery as a whole provides a functional measure of knowledge of current affairs. Overall, results for the five items provide no evidence that newspapers uniquely contribute to knowledge regarding national and international affairs. Cleveland scores exceed marks for the Pittsburgh respondents on four of the items, but the slight differences are unsatisfactory proof that local newspapers affect readers' knowledge levels.[3]

The second battery of knowledge items addresses campaign news, with broad focus on the horse race aspect of the 1992 elections. Questions 6–11 were chosen from a larger item set on the basis of pretest results. This battery performs particularly well, with the percentage of respondents answering the items correctly ranging from 13 percent (item 9) to 86 percent (item 7).[4] Cleveland and Pittsburgh scores are quite similar for all questions in this battery. Hence, we again fail to find evidence that access to a local newspaper influences voters' knowledge levels. However, it is not so obvious what effect should have been expected for the horse race questions. Many analysts have charged that broadcast media dwell on the horse race aspect of campaigns more than do print sources (e.g., Ranney 1983; Patterson and McClure 1976; cf. Sigelman and Bullock 1991). From this perspective, we might expect that Pittsburgh voters, driven toward heightened reliance on broadcast media, would outscore Cleveland respondents on this battery of items. In contrast, we would expect Cleveland respondents to perform best on these and all knowledge items if we hold to the view that the print medium facilitates learning more than do broadcast news sources. Ultimately, the null results of table 4.2 offer support for neither perspective.

Questions 12–17 are about policy positions advanced by the three presidential candidates. With one exception (question 13), these items were drawn from a special series that was run by the Cleveland *Plain Dealer* from late September to election day. Once again, the particular questions included on the postelection survey were determined by pretest results. The *Plain Dealer*'s series presented the candidates' views on a specific issue each day. Each article appeared on a page of section A that was devoted to campaign news. A boxed format, usually titled "Candidates' Views," served to highlight this issue coverage. Figure 4 replicates the *Plain Dealer*'s reporting of the candidates' views on voter registration, the subject of item 15.

Presentation of what became a regular series on the issues seemingly should have helped readers to learn the candidates' views. Likewise, by directly contrasting the three candidates' positions, the issue articles potentially aided voters in distinguishing among the presidential hopefuls. However, viewed more critically, the *Plain Dealer* arguably trivialized important issues by reducing them to a few brief sentences. Further, the absence of analysis of the candidates' statements marks a passive, or objectivity, style of journalism in which the reader receives no context or historical background to help make sense of what the candidates have said (see W. Bennett 1988).

Whatever its hypothetical strengths or weaknesses, the *Plain Dealer*'s issue series apparently did not score a rousing victory in enhancing the information level of the Cleveland electorate. In table 4.2, Cleveland respondents outperformed their Pittsburgh counterparts on only three of the six policy items, and the difference approaches statistical

---

CANDIDATES' VIEWS   voter registration

Should states be required to automatically register people to vote when they apply for drivers' licenses or for government benefits such as unemployment compensation?

PRESIDENT BUSH

"While I strongly support increasing voter participation in the electoral process, I believe requiring states to register people to vote when they apply for drivers' licenses or for government benefits is not the answer. It's critical that states retain their own electoral processes and tailor voter registration procedures to their unique local circumstances."

BILL CLINTON

"I support the so-called motor-voter legislation that would, among other things, allow voters to register when getting their drivers' licenses. Vetoed by the president, this legislation would have helped to increase voter participation. As president, I will sign this legislation."

ROSS PEROT

"First, all of us must vote. We need legislation to make voter registration more accessible. How can anyone disagree?"

Fig. 4. Sample issue coverage in the *Plain Dealer*. (From *Plain Dealer*, October 21, 1992, 4-A.)

significance only for item 17. In short, voters with access to a major local newspaper that specifically highlighted the issues learned nothing more about those issues than did voters who had no newspaper at all. The evidence runs in strong contrast to the oft-stated conclusion that newspapers uniquely contribute to voters' issue awareness.[5]

Results for the issue items might lead us to question whether voters actually learned anything whatsoever about the presidential candidates' policy positions. With three candidates, random guessing on the part of all respondents would produce scores approximating those in table 4.2 for all policy items except for the one concerning Perot's proposed gasoline tax. However, this view is unduly pessimistic. Respondents did not choose randomly among the candidates. A substantial portion of respondents answered "don't know" on the policy items. Hence, of those individuals who offered substantive replies, the portion answering correctly is greater than suggested by the data in table 4.2. Factoring out the "don't know's" most strongly affects results for items 15 and 16, which were answered correctly by 68.4 percent and 70.0 percent of those respondents who chose among the three candidates rather than saying "don't know."

What does the *Plain Dealer*'s coverage tell us about the role of issues in presidential elections? Unfortunately, although stylistic improvements might enhance the utility of the *Plain Dealer*'s issue series, the value of such coverage likely will remain somewhat limited due to the manner in which presidential candidates discuss their policy proposals. For instance, one problem with the "Candidates' Views" series was failure of the two leading candidates to offer decipherable positions on some of the issues. Voters obviously are prevented from evaluating issue positions if those stances are overly vague or incoherent. Consider, for example, Bill Clinton's "response" to a question on health policy:[6]

> *Question:* Do you support needle exchange programs designed to combat AIDS by providing clean hypodermic needles to intravenous drugs users?
> *Clinton:* "We are in the midst of an AIDS and drug epidemic which the current administration has avoided. My administration will demand that drug addicts be treated, and support local communities in their efforts to develop and implement innovative AIDS and drug prevention programs."

Where possible, the *Plain Dealer* attempted to resolve such ambiguity by providing a translation of the candidate's response. However, the following example demonstrates that some answers defy full clarification:[7]

> *Question:* Should the government lift the $10,200 ceiling on how much Americans aged 65 to 70 may earn before their Social Security benefits are reduced?
> *Bush:* "Older Americans should not be discouraged from seeking employment because of the Social Security cap on earnings. I am certainly sympathetic to the concerns expressed by those who call for eliminating the earnings test. I have proposed an earnings test change that balances concerns for the needs of Social Security beneficiaries with constraints imposed by cost considerations." (The administration backs some increase in the earnings test, but objects to raising the tax on Social Security earnings to finance it.)

A second problem with the *Plain Dealer*'s issue coverage is that the candidates often agreed on the issue of the day. For instance, Bush and Clinton offered similar views on the space station, Amtrak, and the B-2 bomber. Likewise, all three of the candidates took essentially identical positions on a question concerning standards for teachers. Candidates do sometimes agree, and the voter undoubtedly learns something when those areas of agreement are highlighted. Nevertheless, indistinguishable policy positions deny the voter a meaningful choice on those policies. If the candidates frequently fail to differ, the vote choice becomes inconsequential as an expression of policy preferences.

A final limitation of the "Campaign Issues" series stems from Ross Perot's failure to offer positions on many of the policy questions. Item 13, which concerns Perot's proposal to increase the gasoline tax, was added to the issue set on the postelection survey because I was unable to find a sufficient number of topics in the "Candidates' Views" series on which Perot offered a position different from those of both George Bush and Bill Clinton.[8] Several installments in the issues series appeared prior to Perot's official entry into the presidential race, and thus he was not requested to provide information for those issues. Further, upon entering the race, Perot declined to present positions on questions about the space station, nuclear weapons tests, endangered species, the Social Security earnings cap, Amtrak, statehood for the District of Columbia, and laws regulating the hiring of replacement workers during labor disputes. Although the voter certainly learns something about a candidate when that candidate is repeatedly nonresponsive to issue queries, the ability to weigh competing policy positions is not enhanced.

Analysis of the *Plain Dealer*'s issue coverage demonstrates the difficulty in conveying clear policy information to voters. Still, the most important point emerging from table 4.2 is that Cleveland and Pittsburgh results for the 17 knowledge items do not differ in any significant or systematic manner. For national and international affairs, it does not appear to be the case that local newspapers have any unique influence on the process of information acquisition. However, examination of results for individual items may fail to detect subtle effects within particular knowledge domains. Note, for example, that Cleveland respondents outscored Pittsburgh respondents on 11 of the 17 knowledge questions, and that the gap approaches statistical significance for 3 of those 11 items. By summing scores within each of the three issue domains, and then comparing Cleveland and Pittsburgh on the resulting measures, we can be certain that no subtle effects have been overlooked.

Cleveland and Pittsburgh scores for the three knowledge batteries are compared in table 4.3. Results mirror those seen earlier for the individual knowledge items. Specifically, there are no differences between Cleveland and Pittsburgh for any knowledge domain. Hence, all evidence points to the same conclusion: access to a major local newspaper neither promotes nor precludes the acquisition of information about current events, campaign news, or candidates' policy positions. Importantly, these results do not mean that there is nothing to be learned from opening a newspaper. Readers undoubtedly do receive information from newspapers. What current results suggest is that that same information can also be acquired elsewhere. In short, local newspapers hold no singular power to foster political awareness, at least for national and international news.

To a large extent, debate over the information value of newspapers pits the local newspaper against broadcast media, and especially television. Results in tables 4.2 and 4.3 demonstrate that the local newspaper offers no unique contribution to the knowledge base of the electorate. However, these findings do not speak directly to the contrast between newspapers and broadcast media. The problem is that other print sources, particularly national newspapers and magazines, are part of the information mix. Pittsburgh respondents suffered no information loss as a result of the local newspaper strike, but we do not know which alternative news sources filled the information gap. In chapter 3, we saw that some Pittsburgh respondents, especially those with high levels of civics knowledge, turned to national print media when local newspapers became unavailable. That reliance on national print sources may account for the absence of an information gap seen in tables 4.2 and 4.3. Thus, it remains possible that local newspapers better inform their audiences than do broadcast media.

We can explore this question further by controlling for the influence of national print media. That is, if we somehow can account for

TABLE 4.3. Knowledge of Current Events, Campaign Facts, and Policy Positions of the Presidential Candidates

	Cuyahoga County	Allegheny County	*t*-value	*N*
Current events	1.205	1.104	1.197	632
Campaign news	3.026	2.991	0.355	631
Presidential candidates' policy positions	2.143	2.073	0.604	633
Total knowledge	6.384	6.161	0.946	629

Note: Cell entries are regional means.

the influence of national print media within the information mix, then the Cleveland versus Pittsburgh comparison essentially will reduce to broadcast media *and* local newspapers (Cleveland) versus only broadcast media (Pittsburgh). Unfortunately, it is not possible to control statistically for the effects of national print media and still maintain the purity of this study's quasi-experimental structure. The problem is that those Pittsburgh respondents who relied on national print media are not a random subset of Pittsburgh voters. Instead, as we saw in chapter 3, individuals with high levels of civics knowledge are particularly likely to turn to national newspapers and magazines for information about the presidential campaign.

There are three relationships to be considered. First, civics knowledge and reliance on national print media are correlated. Second, use of national print media *may* enhance information acquisition. Third, civics knowledge, or political awareness, *does* predict information acquisition. Indeed, we have seen that Price and Zaller (1993) demonstrate quite convincingly that prior political knowledge strongly and consistently predicts news recall. Collectively, these three relationships mean that any effort to control for the effects of national print media on knowledge could throw off this study's de facto randomization by skewing the levels of civics knowledge among the Cleveland and Pittsburgh subsamples. Thus, if an effort is made to control for the impact of national print media, then it is essential to also control for variance in civics knowledge. Identical circumstances demand control for education.

The impact of national print media will be measured with a dummy variable that is coded 1 for those respondents who reported national newspapers or magazines to be one of their top two sources of information about the presidential campaign. This variable is then added to regression models of the form:

$$\text{Current Events Knowledge} = a + b_1\text{Pittsburgh} + b_2\text{Civics}$$

$$\text{Knowledge} + b_3\text{Education} + b_4\text{National Print Media}$$

To recap, the objective is to determine if knowledge levels in Cleveland and Pittsburgh differ after accounting for the influence of national print media. Simultaneous estimation of b_1 and b_4 achieves this end. However, we know that civics knowledge and education are correlated with use of national print media, and that civics knowledge and education both predict information acquisition. Thus, these variables must be included in the statistical models, or else the coefficient for national print media will be artificially inflated. That bias would affect the estimate for the

Pittsburgh versus Cleveland contrast, and thus would preclude assessment of the impact of local newspapers on information acquisition.

Regression estimates are depicted in table 4.4. The Pittsburgh dummy variable represents the impact of living in a region where local newspapers are not available, controlling for the influence of national print media. Thus, in essence, this variable contrasts the effect of access to only broadcast media (Pittsburgh) with the effect of access to both broadcast media and local newspapers (Cleveland). Unfortunately, this test is neither as pure nor as simple as the previous quasi-experimental comparisons. The methodological circumstances resemble those of the cross-sectional studies discussed earlier; assessment of the direction of causality can be only speculative if experimental manipulations are

TABLE 4.4. Regional Variance in Political Knowledge, with Control
for Use of National Print Media

	Dependent Variable		
	Current Events	Campaign News	Policy Positions
Constant	-0.119	1.673****	0.842****
	(-0.948)	(10.798)	(4.542)
Pittsburgh	-0.098	-0.075	-0.090
	(-1.332)	(-0.804)	(-0.839)
Civics knowledge	0.390****	0.435****	0.389****
	(12.482)	(11.405)	(8.485)
Education	0.060***	0.050*	0.054*
	(2.817)	(1.923)	(1.703)
National print media	0.329**	-0.379	0.582***
	(2.596)	(-1.399)	(3.123)
Pittsburgh x national print media	—	0.748**	—
		(2.304)	
N	629	628	629
R^2	.265	.216	.155
Change in R^2	.008	.007	.013

Note: The "change in R^2" statistic indicates the improvement in model performance that comes with adding the national print media terms to models that include only Pittsburgh, civics knowledge, and education.

t-values are in parentheses.

* $p < .10$, ** $p < .05$, *** $p < .01$, **** $p < .001$

unavailable. Nevertheless, the results in table 4.4 are quite striking: even after controlling for the impact of national print media, access to a major local newspaper has no affect on knowledge of current events, campaign news, or candidates' policy positions. In short, no evidence has been found to suggest that local newspapers hold any advantage over broadcast media as information sources for news about national or international events.

Civics knowledge emerges as an extremely strong and impressively consistent predictor of information acquisition. This finding corroborates Price and Zaller's (1993) point that prior political knowledge outperforms competing variables as a measure of media exposure. Education also functions as a highly consistent predictor of knowledge, but the effect is much weaker than that of civics knowledge. Finally, results for the national print media dummy variable are mixed. For all respondents, reliance on national print media predicts both current events knowledge and knowledge of the presidential candidates' policy positions (for these dependent variables, the national print media × Pittsburgh interactions were insignificant). In contrast, reliance on national print sources increased knowledge of campaign events only for Pittsburgh respondents. Although the impact of national print media provides some support for a specialized version of the print superiority thesis, too much should not be made of this point. The "change in R^2" statistic at the bottom of each column in table 4.4 indicates the improvement in model performance when the national print media variables are added to a model including only the Pittsburgh dummy variable, civics knowledge, and education. These scores are extremely slight, providing further evidence for the point made previously by Price and Zaller (1993) and Neuman, Just, and Crigler (1992): characteristics of the person drive information acquisition far more than do characteristics of the medium.

Do We Know What We Know?

Subjective and objective measures of political knowledge have been introduced to explore the influence of local newspapers on information acquisition. With that task now accomplished, it may be informative to diverge briefly in order to examine the relationship between the two sets of knowledge measures. At question is whether a correlation exists linking self-reported political knowledge and the objective indicators of political awareness. The answer to this question will be revealing on two levels. First, evidence of correlation between the subjective and objective measures would help to establish the validity of the self-report data.

The greatest potential limitation of respondents' self-reports stems from the fact that those assessments may have little or no basis in empirical reality. In other words, voters' perceptions regarding their levels of awareness do not necessarily bear any resemblance to those voters' actual levels of awareness. If this were the case, conclusions drawn from analysis of the self-report data would be seriously undermined.

Second, on a more substantive level, study of the correlation between subjective and objective knowledge measures may provide insight into the psyche of the American voter. For example, if voters with low scores on the objective indicators are aware that their political knowledge is minimal, a plausible interpretation would be that apathy pervades the electorate. Conversely, the absence of a correlation between the objective and subjective measures would indicate that voters misjudge the extent to which they are informed. In this case, voters might possess the motivation necessary to obtain additional information about political candidates, yet not recognize how much additional information is available.

The Pearson correlation matrix depicted in table 4.5 includes seven variables: the three self-report items, the scales constructed from the

TABLE 4.5. The Relationship between Self-Reported and Objective Measures of Political Knowledge (Pearson correlation matrix)

	Pres.	Senate	House	Civics	Current Events	Campaign News	Policy Positions
Self-reported presidential	1.000	0.348	0.327	0.165	0.174	0.130	0.146
Self-reported Senate	0.348	1.000	0.486	0.203	0.190	0.122	0.172
Self-reported House	0.327	0.486	1.000	0.164	0.108	0.081	0.077
Civics knowledge	0.165	0.203	0.164	1.000	0.491	0.453	0.365
Current events	0.174	0.190	0.108	0.491	1.000	0.410	0.463
Campaign news	0.130	0.122	0.081	0.453	0.410	1.000	0.388
Policy positions	0.146	0.172	0.077	0.365	0.463	0.388	1.000

three batteries of knowledge items, and civics knowledge. All scores are statistically significant, but the magnitude of the correlations varies dramatically, from 0.077 to 0.491. The average correlation among the three self-report items is 0.387, suggesting that voters perceive a relationship in their levels of awareness concerning different electoral campaigns. Similarly, the average correlation among the three batteries of objective items is 0.420, and the average correlation between these batteries and civics knowledge is 0.436; some variance exists across knowledge domains, but those persons who are well informed in one area generally tend to be well informed in other areas.

The average correlation between the objective and subjective measures is 0.133. This score defies simple interpretation. It is clearly the case that individuals who think that they know a great deal about political affairs do indeed tend to score the highest on the objective tests. However, the relationship between objective and subjective measures is also less than overwhelming in strength. To some extent, this should be expected. First, the subjective questions asked respondents how much they knew about the candidates, but made no reference to either the horse race aspect of the campaigns or to candidates' policy positions. Voters may know a great deal about a candidate's background, experience, personality, and so on, yet not know many details concerning policy proposals. Second, the objective measures primarily involved the presidential campaign, which means that it is understandable if weak correlations link these scales and self-reports for the House and Senate elections. This is especially true for the House measure, because this item was alone among the knowledge indicators in that scores varied by region as a consequence of Pittsburgh's newspaper strike.

The correlations between the presidential self-report item and the objective measures add little clarity. Although the horse race and policy questions primarily concern the presidential election, the scales formed from these questions are correlated equally strongly with the presidential and Senate self-report questions. Further, the self-report scores are correlated more strongly with the current events scale than with either of the two campaign-specific indicators. Hence, voters may possess a general recognition of their own levels of political awareness, but this understanding apparently is too blunt to capture subtle domain-specific distinctions.

The existence of significant correlations bolsters the claim that self-report items provide valid indicators of political awareness. We can have some confidence in these measures, particularly when they are used for purposes such as the one in this chapter, where the subjective measures are employed only to explore aggregate regional effects. Unfortunately, insight regarding the American voter is less clear. If the subjective and objective measures were highly correlated, we could conclude that a large body of apathetic voters recognize and tolerate their own lack of political awareness. However, the weak correlations depicted in table 4.5 simply do not support such a conclusion. Voters possess only a general sense of how much they know, which leaves open the possibility that voters hold the motivation necessary to acquire greater quantities of campaign information.

Conclusion

Due to a newspaper strike, residents of the Pittsburgh area lived for eight months without access to a major local newspaper. The evidence presented in this chapter reveals that this lack of access to print media brought strikingly little influence on the ability of Pittsburgh residents to keep informed about national and international politics. The absence of local newspapers had no effect on any objective indicator of political awareness, whether it be an individual fact or a knowledge domain. Further, control for exposure to national print media failed to alter results, suggesting that local newspapers hold no advantage over broadcast media in informing the public. Likewise, survey respondents did not perceive the absence of a local newspaper to have any adverse effect on their ability to stay informed about the 1992 presidential and Senate campaigns. Cumulatively, the evidence is shattering for any theory of print superiority.

Newspapers may exert no unique influence on the information base of the American electorate, but this does not suggest that media are irrelevant. Media *do* matter. When voters live in a media-poor environment, as Pittsburgh's House voters did in 1992, knowledge levels decline. Hence, contrary to minimal-effects views of media, the dynamics of political behavior are affected by media exposure (see also Bartels 1993). However, these same dynamics are not affected by the particular medium from which the voter receives the news. The importance of local newspapers is not some mystical capacity to convey a deep understanding of factual information. Instead, the local newspaper is important because it often is the only medium to provide coverage of local politics. If broadcast media fail to report on U.S. House races, then it is safe to assume that they fare even worse for most municipal and county elections.

For many analysts, it will remain troubling that American citizens demonstrate a consistently poor understanding of the basic facts of government. Recent evidence that individuals routinely simplify political decision making through application of heuristic principles of judgment should provide some comfort (e.g., Popkin 1991; Sniderman, Brody, and Tetlock 1991). Still, few would argue that a better informed public would be undesirable. Unfortunately, the prescription for that end remains elusive. The easy answer is to blame the citizen. People just don't care enough about politics. People won't even read a newspaper. However, this chapter suggests that the easy answer is also the wrong answer on two counts. First, people do care about politics. Apathy surely exists, but it does not pervade the American electorate. This study's voters desired to acquire information about the 1992 elections, and they perceived themselves to be relatively well informed about those contests. Second, television is not the culprit, and newspapers are not the savior. If we truly desire to increase the knowledge levels of voters, the most immediate returns will be gained by improving the clarity with which issues are debated by candidates, and reported by media.

CHAPTER 5

News Media and Political Discussion

You got news for me
I got nothing for you
—John Prine

Information plays a central role in any plausible model of electoral decision making, because what the voter knows about the candidates will
influence what the voter decides regarding which candidate to support.
Although news media provide much of the new information voters receive over the course of a political campaign, social networks also transmit political information (e.g., Huckfeldt 1986; Huckfeldt and Sprague
1987; Huckfeldt and Sprague 1995). Interpersonal discussion is one possible avenue for social influence; when talk turns to politics, political behavior may be affected. Interpersonal discussion may disseminate information about campaigns, and discussion partners may attempt to influence
one another's electoral choices. Consequently, full understanding of the
dynamics of information acquisition in U.S. elections requires attention
to the possible role played by social channels of communication.

In this chapter, the relationship between news media and interpersonal political discussion is explored. Impressive bodies of research have
contributed separately to our understanding of the importance of news
media in political campaigns, and to our understanding of the role of
social influence within those same campaigns. However, progress has
been less rapid in detailing how news media and social influence relate
to one another (Ansolabehere, Behr, and Iyengar 1991; Chaffee and
Mutz 1988). Instead, many studies of news media effects ignore the
surrounding social context, and, likewise, many studies concerning the
dynamics of social influence do not consider how news media contribute
to that influence. Perhaps the most basic question is whether the relationship between news media and social influence is conflicting or complementary (Chaffee and Mutz 1988). For example, do some voters choose
to receive campaign information from news media rather than through
interpersonal discussion, or does the information voters acquire from
news media become the raw material for subsequent conversations
about politics? A related question is whether news media and interpersonal discussion exert interacting influence on electoral choice. If political discussion is inherently persuasive in content, then that persuasive

force may be strengthened or weakened when voters acquire additional information from a media-rich decision-making context.

Media Access and Political Discussion

The Pittsburgh newspaper strike facilitates study of the link between media access and political discussion. The postelection survey includes a battery of items designed specifically to measure various aspects of respondents' discussion networks. Therefore, it will be possible to determine if discussion is affected by the quantity of electoral information made available by news media. Ultimately, we may gain new perspective on the question of whether the relationship between media and discussion is conflicting or complementary.

A degree of methodological caution is required when assessing the link between media and discussion. The quantity and character of mass and interpersonal communication are not directly comparable. For example, the information value of an hour of political discussion may be very different from the value of one hour of televised news (see Chaffee and Mutz 1988). Unfortunately, this lack of a common denominator complicates efforts to measure the relative importance of media and discussion for American electoral behavior. However, three aspects of this study's design help to diminish the severity of this problem. First, the analysis in this chapter will focus primarily on the direction rather than the magnitude of effects. That is, my objective is simply to determine if media access exerts positive or negative influence on political discussion. Second, most of the media and discussion variables use a common scale. Although this design feature does not ensure comparability of results, it does at least reduce the problem of disparity in measurement. Third, rather than treating political discussion as monolithic, I will examine the relationship between media access and several specific aspects of discussant relationships. This strategy minimizes the risk that a subtle link between media and discussion will be overlooked.

Initially, the analysis will focus on three elements of discussant relationships. First, I will consider whether media access affects the sheer quantity of interpersonal discussion. The second question is whether the media context influences respondents' perceptions of their discussants. For example, is the discussant viewed as more or less knowledgeable when media access is constrained? The third topic is the content of political discussion. More specifically, do media reports direct the particular subjects that acquaintances discuss? These initial questions concern the actual dynamics of discussion. Later, we will consider the effects of discussion by examining the relationship between media, political discussion, and the vote choice.

The search for media effects requires comparison of discussion data from the Cleveland and Pittsburgh subsamples. We have seen that the two subsamples are statistically indistinct on a host of individual-level political and demographic characteristics, suggesting that those factors can be ruled out as determinants of regional variance in political discussion. Further, we have seen that the Pittsburgh newspaper strike affected general levels of media access for the House races to a far greater extent than for the Senate or presidential campaigns. Thus, it will be possible to determine if access to local newspapers uniquely affects political discussion through examination of data for the Senate and presidential elections, while more general media effects will be considered with data concerning this study's six U.S. House elections.

The Quantity of Political Discussion

Studies investigating the relationship between news media and interpersonal discussion typically examine the extent to which media exposure and discussion covary (e.g., Wanta and Wu 1992). Unfortunately, such an approach does not aid in identifying causal links because we do not know what factor—media, discussion, both media and discussion, or a third covariate—drives the identified relationship. However, if we can experimentally induce variance in either media exposure or discussion, then we gain some capacity to speak to the direction of causality. For example, if news media and interpersonal discussion compete as sources of electoral information (e.g., Erbring, Goldenberg, and Miller 1980), then a reduction in media access should increase the frequency of political discussion. Conversely, if news reports generate some of the topics of political discussion (e.g., Katz and Feldman 1962; Beck 1991), then discussion should decline in response to decreased access to news media. This study's quasi-experimental design brings the methodological leverage needed to pursue the question of causality.

Two groups of questions concerning political discussion were included on the postelection survey. Initially, several items measured respondents' general patterns of political discussion. Following these questions, respondents were asked to provide the first name of the one person with whom they had discussed politics the most over the course of the 1992 campaign season. Several subsequent questions explored respondents' perceptions of the discussion partners they named. These items are designed to allow analysis of how media access relates to specific discussant relationships, and also to facilitate study of the link between social communication and electoral choice.

Three survey questions provide data regarding the amount of political discussion reported by the Pittsburgh and Cleveland respondents. The first two items measure the total quantity of discussion; the first question asks respondents to gauge the amount of discussion they had concerning the 1992 elections, and the second question directs respondents to compare 1992 discussion levels with those for prior election years. The third item measures the frequency with which respondents talked about politics with their self-reported main discussants. Again, comparison of Cleveland and Pittsburgh data enables estimation of the impact of media access on the quantity of political discussion.

Results reported in table 5.1 reveal that differences in the quantity of political discussion in Pittsburgh and Cleveland are negligible and statistically indistinct. The discussion variables are coded using four- and five-point scales, yet regional variance in discussion is less than a tenth of a point on all three measures. The Pittsburgh newspaper strike apparently exerted no influence on the frequency of interpersonal political discussion.

Recall that Pittsburgh-area voters succeeded in finding acceptable substitutes for local newspapers for news concerning the presidential and

TABLE 5.1. The Quantity of Political Discussion

	Cuyahoga County	Allegheny County	t-value	N
Amount of discussion	2.362	2.441	-1.203	633
Amount vs. previous election years	2.974	3.059	-1.027	627
Frequency of conversation with top discussant	1.952	2.045	-1.326	602

Note: Cell entries are regional means. Data are drawn from three questions: (1) "Some people talk about political elections with friends, relatives, coworkers, and other acquaintances. How much discussion would you say you have had about this year's elections. Would you say a great deal, some, only a little, or none at all?" Results are coded 0 (none at all) to 3 (a great deal); (2) Compared to previous election years, how much would you say you've discussed politics this year. Would you say a great deal more than in other years, somewhat more, about the same, somewhat less, or a great deal less?" Results are coded 0 (a great deal less) to 4 (a great deal more); (3) "When you talk with (name of person respondent spoke with the most about the events of the election year), about how often did you discuss politics. Would you say every day, one or twice a week, once or twice a month, or less than that?" Results are coded 0 (less than once a month) to 3 (every day).

Senate elections. Because the newspaper strike did not affect media attentiveness for those contests, and because the discussion data reported in
table 5.1 are not contest-specific, we cannot conclude that media exposure and political discussion are unrelated. Instead, these findings reveal
only that access to local newspapers exerts no unique influence on the
quantity of political discussion. In short, if media exposure does influence
levels of political discussion, it apparently makes no difference whether or
not local newspapers are part of the news context. If media reports fuel
political discussion, then discussion seemingly runs just as well on broadcast or national print media as on the coverage provided by local newspapers. Similarly, if media exposure is an obstacle to interpersonal discussion, that barrier is not weakened by the absence of local newspapers.
This finding reinforces the point that voters generally are able to cope
quite well with the absence of newspapers. Most of the statewide, national, and international information voters receive from local newspapers is available elsewhere, and thus the lack of access to newspapers
brings little or no effect on the quantity of political discussion.

The Perceived Quality of Discussant Relationships

The possibility that interpersonal discussion affects political judgments
arguably hinges on the assumption that individuals view their discussants
as reliable sources of information about politics. Put another way, if
discussion provides cues to efficiency-minded voters (Popkin 1991), then
the impact of discussion may vary as a function of the persuasive
strength of those cues. Discussion may be irrelevant if individuals consider their discussants' political judgments to be ill founded or incompe-
tent (cf. Huckfeldt and Sprague 1991).

Media exposure potentially affects voters' judgments concerning
the quality of their discussant relationships in two distinct ways. Initially,
if respondents assess the political knowledge or attentiveness of discussants relative to their own knowledge or attentiveness, then diminished media access may improve the perceived standing of discussants.
From this perspective, it is not how much the discussant knows that
matters, but how much more than the respondent the discussant knows.
Lacking access to news media, the respondent feels somewhat uninformed, and thus overvalues a discussant's political competence. Alternatively, a political context thirsty for news may produce uninformed
discussants. If the discussant acquires information from news media,
then this discussant will provide the respondent with little electoral insight when news reports become scarce. Consequently, the respondent
may perceive the discussant to be relatively uninformed about politics.

Data are drawn from three questions concerning respondents' perceptions of their main discussants. These items measure discussants' attentiveness to the 1992 elections, discussants' general knowledge about politics, and the frequency with which respondents and discussants disagree.[1] Results depicted in table 5.2 indicate that Pittsburgh and Cleveland respondents are quite similar in their perceptions of the quality of discussant relationships. Cleveland and Pittsburgh data are essentially identical for the second and third items; in contrast, the difference in results for the first item approaches statistical significance. Although this effect indicates that Pittsburgh-area voters may have had more positive perceptions of their discussants than voters from Cleveland, a cautious interpretation is warranted. First, the difference is substantively trivial, representing less than a tenth of a point on a four-point scale. Second, respondents from both regions reported their discussants to be highly attentive to the 1992 elections, suggesting that discussants in both Cleveland and Pittsburgh meet any reasonable competence threshold.

These results indicate that access to local newspapers exerts no unique influence on the quality of discussant relationships. It apparently is not the case, for instance, that discussants must draw obscure political trivia from the local newspaper to dazzle their friends and acquaintances. Whatever general contribution newspapers make to the quantity

TABLE 5.2. Respondents' Perceptions of Discussion Partners

	Cuyahoga County	Allegheny County	t-value	N
Discussant's attentiveness to elections	2.644	2.724	-1.658*	586
Discussant's knowledge about politics	2.411	2.466	-1.001	591
Frequency of disagreement	1.731	1.766	-0.492	591

Note: Cell entries are regional means. Data are drawn from three questions: (1) "How much attention do you think (name of person respondent spoke with the most about the events of the election year) gave to this year's elections. Would you say a great deal, some, only a little, or none at all?" Results are coded 0 (none at all) to 3 (a great deal); (2) And, generally speaking, how much do you think (name) knows about politics. Would you say a great deal, some, only a little, or none at all?" Results are coded 0 (none at all) to 3 (a great deal); (3) "When you talk about politics with (name), how often do you disagree. Would you say often, sometimes, rarely, or never?" Results are coded 0 (never) to 3 (often).
    * $p < .10$

or quality of interpersonal political discussion can also be acquired from alternative media sources. Of course, despite the absence of evidence that newspapers alter the general nature of discussant relationships, it remains possible that media exposure affects the specific content of political discussion.

Topics of Discussion

Denied access to their major local newspapers, residents of the Pittsburgh area were able to find acceptable substitute news sources for the presidential and Senate races, but not for the U.S. House campaigns. Hence, the quasi-experimental manipulation was most successful in limiting media exposure for the congressional contests, suggesting that specific study of interpersonal discussion concerning those elections may provide the best opportunity to identify the relationship between media access and political discussion. If discussion is affected by media exposure, then Cleveland and Pittsburgh data should exhibit a different pattern for the House elections than for other possible topics of discussion.

Survey respondents were asked to report their levels of interpersonal discussion about four specific topics: issues; the presidential campaign; the Senate campaign; and the U.S. House campaign in each voter's district. Results are shown in table 5.3. Looking first at the

TABLE 5.3. Topics of Political Discussion

	Cuyahoga County	Allegheny County	t-value	N
Issues	2.495	2.480	0.236	632
Presidential election	2.511	2.549	-0.624	631
Senate election	1.536	1.767	-3.342*	634
House election	1.580	1.243	4.526**	632

Note: Cell entries are regional means. Data are drawn from the following questions: "Political discussion can focus on various topics. For each of the following, please tell me if you talked about it a great deal, some, only a little, or none at all. First, what about issues (such as the economy and foreign policy)? Second, what about the presidential election? And this year's Senate election? And this year's congressional election in your district?" Results are coded 0 (none at all) to 3 (a great deal).
* $p < .01$, ** $p < .001$

Cleveland, or Cuyahoga County, data, we see clear evidence that respondents did not treat all potential topics of political discussion equally. Cell means for discussion about issues and about the presidential election fall midway between "a great deal" and "some" discussion; in contrast, mean scores for the Senate and House elections are a full point lower on the four-point scale, falling between "some" and "only a little" discussion. Although these results are not surprising, they do establish that respondents are able to differentiate among topics of political discussion, and that the most salient topics generate the highest levels of discussion.

In table 5.3, Cleveland and Pittsburgh results do not differ for the first two topics of discussion, issues and the presidential election. In contrast, Pittsburgh respondents report relatively high levels of discussion about Pennsylvania's Senate race, and relatively low levels of discussion about the local U.S. House campaigns. This curious pattern of results seemingly indicates that media exposure does influence the content of political discussion, although the nature of this relationship may not be immediately obvious due to the conflicting findings for the Senate and House elections.

Beginning with the House data, we see that the Cleveland and Pittsburgh means are separated by a gap of 0.337 points, and that the difference in means is highly significant. Because of the newspaper strike, residents of the Pittsburgh area had access to little information about the local congressional elections. Voters found few alternatives to their missing local newspapers, meaning that the strike significantly affected media access for the congressional races. Lacking relevant news, voters in Pittsburgh largely neglected to discuss their local House campaigns. The clear implication is that media exposure *fuels* political discussion; if the availability of news reports about a topic is limited, corresponding discussion of that topic declines in response. However, although the effect is statistically significant, it is less than overwhelming in magnitude. Voters in Pittsburgh did not discuss their House elections as frequently as did voters in Cleveland, but some level of discussion apparently can occur even when the information context is quite media-poor.

Can we conclude with confidence that a *causal* relationship has been identified? That is, can we be certain that some force other than media exposure is not driving the Cleveland versus Pittsburgh effect? Three factors support the conclusion that media exposure exerts positive influence on political discussion. First, results in table 5.3 mirror media attentiveness data reported in chapter 3; for the House elections, Pittsburgh respondents were less attentive to media than Cleveland respondents by a margin of 0.348 points, an effect nearly matched by the 0.337-

point gap in discussion in table 5.3. Second, political discussion was minimal in Pittsburgh only for the topic for which news reports were lacking, the local congressional elections. Conversely, levels of discussion in Pittsburgh matched or exceeded those in Cleveland for all topics for which exposure to news was not constrained, topics including the Senate and presidential campaigns. Hence, if a factor other than media exposure is driving this effect, it is a factor that operates exclusively on a single component of political discussion. Third, the inclusion of multiple congressional districts provides a safeguard against confusing regional variance with district-specific effects. Separate tests demonstrate that the means for each of the three Pennsylvania districts differ significantly from the Cuyahoga County mean.[2] Further, paired comparisons contrasting results for each of the three Pennsylvania contests with each of the three Ohio races reveal higher levels of discussion in the Ohio districts for eight of the nine comparisons.[3] Such consistent effects can only be reasonably attributed to the decline in media exposure induced by the Pittsburgh newspaper strike.

Results in table 5.3 also indicate that Pennsylvania's Senate race was a more popular topic of political discussion than was Ohio's Senate election. The most plausible explanation for this disparity centers on the campaigns themselves. As we have seen, Ohio's Senate race was relatively nondescript, and was not much of a contest in Cuyahoga County. In contrast, Pennsylvania's Specter-Yeakel election was decided by narrow margins both statewide and within Allegheny County. Also, recall that the Pennsylvania candidates combined to spend nearly twice as much as their counterparts in Ohio. Thus, it is not surprising that this hotly contested race prompted more discussion than Ohio's Glenn-DeWine election, particularly given the earlier evidence that the media attentiveness of Pittsburgh's Senate voters was not adversely affected by the newspaper strike.

The conventional wisdom regarding media in presidential campaigns holds that newspapers provide more detailed issue coverage than do broadcast media (e.g., Owen 1991; Davis 1992). Indeed, some analysts have provided harsh criticism of television's campaign coverage (e.g., Patterson and McClure 1976; Patterson 1980). However, current results conflict with the conventional wisdom. The data in table 5.3 regarding levels of discussion about the presidential campaign suggest that voters discuss issues primarily in the context of presidential politics. In both Cleveland and Pittsburgh, the issue and presidential election means are virtually identical. What is noteworthy is that the absence of a major local newspaper did not preclude issue discussion in Pittsburgh. This finding bolsters one of chapter 4's central conclusions:

local newspapers play no unique role in informing voters about campaign issues at the national level.

The most important finding regarding the relationship between media exposure and political discussion emerges from the House data in table 5.3. The low level of discussion by Pittsburgh-area voters about the congressional campaigns indicates that media provide at least some of the raw material for political discussion. However, an important question remains: does media exposure affect the influence of political discussion on electoral choice? That is, do discussant effects on the vote choice presuppose specific discussion about the campaign in question?

Political Discussion and the Vote

Pittsburgh's newspaper strike did not prevent voters from engaging in political discussion, but the strike did limit discussion concerning one specific topic, the local U.S. House races. New evidence regarding the dynamics of political discussion is important in itself, but the significance of this evidence will be magnified if it contributes to our understanding of electoral choice. Three specific questions will be examined. First, and most basic, does political discussion affect the vote choice? Second, if discussion does affect the vote choice, must the voter first discuss the campaign in question for that influence to occur? And third, does media access moderate discussant influence on electoral choice?

The central independent variable, discussant partisanship (DPID), is constructed using data from two questions concerning respondents' perceptions of their main discussants. Respondents were asked if their discussants normally support candidates who are Democrats or Republicans, and also which candidate their discussants supported in the 1992 presidential race. Hence, DPID = 2 (respondent believes that discussant normally supports candidates who are Democrats, and that discussant voted for Clinton in 1992) to -2 (respondent believes that discussant normally supports candidates who are Republicans, and that discussant voted for Bush in 1992).[4]

The study of discussant effects on electoral choice brings several methodological difficulties (Huckfeldt and Sprague 1991; Berelson, Lazarsfeld, and McPhee 1954). First, the measure of discussant partisanship draws on respondents' perceptions rather than the self-reports of the discussants themselves. This raises the possibility that respondents have misperceived their discussants' political predispositions, perhaps by imputing to the discussants their own electoral preferences. Although this risk is genuine, it does not obscure study of discussant effects on electoral choice. Huckfeldt and Sprague (1991) examine the impact of discussants' self-reported presidential votes on the corresponding presidential votes of the main respondents, and find that perception drives discussant effects. When main respondents misperceive their discussants' political preferences, the actual preferences exert no influence on the political judgments of the main respondents. Hence, to examine the influence of political discussion on the political behavior of the respondent, we must view that discussion through the respondent's eyes. Consequently, no methodological harm results from using respondents' perceptions to construct the measure of discussant partisanship.

Second, similarity in the electoral preferences of respondents and discussants may reflect a shared understanding of politics rather than true discussant influence (Huckfeldt and Sprague 1991). If discussion partners are exposed to similar social and political forces outside of the discussant relationship, those forces may produce commonality in electoral preference. In other words, respondents and discussants may independently construct identical vote choices, creating the incorrect appearance of discussant influence. To guard against this possibility, variables will be included in all statistical models to account for critical individual-level factors that may affect the respondent's vote choice.

Third, discussion effects may be bidirectional. A correlation between discussant partisanship and the electoral behavior of the respondents may indicate that discussants exerted influence on the respondents, but it is also conceivable that the correlation reflects the influence of respondents on their discussants. Although this possible simultaneity is troublesome, the influence of political discussion within individual dyads appears to be essentially unidirectional. For example, Huckfeldt and Sprague (1991) find that within nonrelative dyads, only 15 percent of the relationships include two individuals who each named the other when asked to identify political discussants. Hence, the risk that simultaneity will result in misspecification of discussant effects is minimal.

A final methodological concern is possible simultaneity between a respondent's vote choice and partisanship. Many studies employ a seven-point measure of partisanship when estimating vote choice. However, Franklin and Jackson (1983) demonstrate that the vote choice affects self-reported partisanship. For example, a voter answering a postelection survey may claim to be a strong rather than weak Republican as a consequence of the electoral choices the voter made in that year's elections. Stated most forcefully, Fiorina (1979, 97) argues that the seven-point indicator is "hopelessly polluted." If we were to ignore self-reported party identification, the impact of discussant partisanship undoubtedly would be artificially inflated, yet the conventional seven-point measure brings its own unique complications. Huckfeldt and

Sprague (1991) address this problem by introducing a three-category measure of respondent partisanship, with dummy variables used to differentiate self-identified Democrats, Republicans, and independents. That procedure will be repeated here.

In addition to the partisanship dummy variables, the statistical models include a measure of respondents' self-reported ideology (0 = strong conservative to 6 = strong liberal). Further, in models of the House vote, two dummy variables identify the six House contests by incumbency status, distinguishing seats defended by Democratic incumbents from the study's open seat and the seat defended by a Republican incumbent (Open = 1 if Ohio's Nineteenth District and 0 if otherwise; IncR = 1 if Pennsylvania's Eighteenth District and 0 if otherwise). Because voters in open-seat districts are particularly likely to draw on simple voting cues (Mondak 1993b; Mondak and McCurley 1994), an interaction term is included to account for the possibility that the predictive power of partisanship will be greatest when a district's incumbent declines to seek reelection.[5]

Logit estimates for three discussant effects models are depicted in table 5.4. The dependent variables are coded 1 if the respondent voted for the Democratic candidate, and 0 if the respondent voted for the Republican nominee; Perot voters are omitted from the model of the presidential vote. Results for partisanship and ideology are as expected: in all cases, the probability of a Democratic vote declines if the respondent is an independent or Republican rather than a Democrat, and if the respondent is conservative or moderate rather than liberal. Note that the effects of partisanship and ideology diminish in magnitude as we move from the presidential vote to the Senate vote, and from the Senate vote to the House vote. Additionally, results in the third column of table 5.4 indicate that the impact of partisanship on the House vote is approximately twice as strong in the study's open seat as in those districts defended by incumbents.

Discussant partisanship exerts strong and statistically significant influence on the presidential and House votes. Further, inclusion of the discussant partisanship variable appears to produce an improvement in model performance versus models in which this variable is excluded. The precise magnitude of this improvement cannot be specified due to the absence of an accepted goodness-of-fit measure for logistic regression (see Agresti 1990; Demaris 1992). However, a simple indicator of improvement in model performance is provided by the difference between the model chi-squares for models that do and do not include the variable in question. This statistic follows a chi-square distribution with one degree of freedom. Here, the addition to chi-square is significant at

$p < .001$ for both the presidential and House models. In contrast with results for the presidential and House votes, the effect of discussant partisanship on the Senate vote is marginal, and fails to reach statistical significance. The addition to chi-square for this model likewise falls short of conventional levels of statistical significance.

Figure 5 depicts the impact of discussant partisanship on the estimated probability of a Democratic vote (independent = 1; ideology = 3; IncR, Open, and Pittsburgh = 0). Discussant partisanship produces a swing of over 50 points in the probability of a Democratic presidential vote, and a swing of nearly 30 points in the probability of a Democratic

TABLE 5.4. The Influence of Political Discussion on Electoral Choice

	Presidential	Senate	House
Constant	1.286** (3.390)	1.284** (4.543)	0.752* (2.666)
Republican	-3.786** (-9.429)	-2.634** (-8.382)	-1.911** (-6.342)
Independent	-1.752** (-4.836)	-1.334** (-5.032)	-1.187** (-4.564)
Ideology	0.362** (4.063)	0.304** (4.920)	0.093 (1.622)
IncR	—	—	-1.355** (-4.448)
Open	—	—	1.375* (2.962)
Republican x open	—	—	-2.091* (-2.847)
Pittsburgh	0.135 (0.437)	-1.579** (-6.639)	0.101 (0.398)
Discussant PID	0.658** (5.816)	0.130 (1.514)	0.294** (3.751)
N	471	542	538
Model chi-square	326.795	244.925	187.167

Note: Dependent variables are the two-party vote, coded 1 if respondent voted Democratic, 0 if respondent voted Republican; *t*-values are in parentheses.
 * $p < .01$, ** $p < .001$

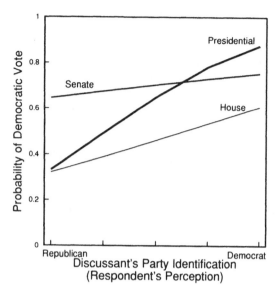

Fig. 5. Political discussion and electoral choice. (Data from table 5.4.)

House vote. However, the probability of a Democratic Senate vote varies by only 10 points across discussant partisanship. The sizable effects for the presidential and House votes are particularly impressive because the discussant partisanship variable incorporates perceptions regarding only one discussion partner per respondent. If the voter discusses politics with several individuals, and if that discussion produces consistent political signals, we should expect the full impact of interpersonal discussion to exceed the level of influence portrayed in figure 5.

The influence of discussion on electoral choice shows considerable variance in strength for the presidential, Senate, and House elections. This variance coupled with the existence of discussant influence on the House vote despite generally low levels of topic-specific communication raises a question concerning the decision-making mechanism underlying discussant effects. If explicit persuasion leads to social influence, then the impact of political discussion should increase as a function of the quantity of discourse (Latane 1981). From this perspective, political discussion characterized by frequent and vigorous direct appeals brings the greatest probability of producing discussant effects. In contrast with this social cohesion model, the structural equivalence model holds that individuals search for behavioral cues by examining the relevant beliefs of other persons in common structural situations (Burt 1987). The structural equivalence model posits that discussant influence presupposes neither frequent contact nor outwardly persuasive discussion. Instead, provided that an individual can ascertain the political predispositions of acquaintances, those predispositions can guide the individual's subsequent political behavior (see also Huckfeldt and Sprague 1991).

Data regarding the quantity of discussion provide the opportunity to explore which mechanism underlies discussant influence on the vote choice. Recall that respondents were asked to what extent they discussed their presidential, Senate, and House campaigns, and how frequently they talked about politics with their main discussion partners. By interacting these variables with discussant partisanship, it will be possible to determine whether discussant effects on vote choice grow stronger as a function of the frequency of relevant discussion. Significant positive interactions would be consistent with the social cohesion model, whereas the absence of significant interactions would be consistent with the structural equivalence model.

Results are depicted in tables 5.5 and 5.6. Consistent effects emerge in table 5.5, where we see that discussant influence on vote choice is not contingent on the frequency of interaction between discussion partners. Although the signs of the interaction terms are in the direction predicted by the social cohesion model for the presidential and House votes, the coefficients are weak. Likewise, the interaction term's coefficient for the Senate model is essentially zero. Hence, it appears that discussant effects on vote choice do not require that discussion partners talk about politics with any great frequency. Similarly, results in table 5.6 reveal that the influence of discussant partisanship does not increase as a function of the quantity of topic-specific communication. In fact, the interaction term for the Senate model produces a marginally significant ($p <$ .10) *negative* coefficient, suggesting that discussant influence on the Senate vote may be weakest among those individuals who discussed their Senate elections the most. Also, because frequency of discussion about the House races does not moderate discussant influence on the congressional vote, the reduction in topic-specific discussion caused by Pittsburgh's newspaper strike brings no corresponding impact on the vote.

The absence of significant positive interactions in tables 5.5 and 5.6 runs contrary to the expectations of the social cohesion perspective. Discussant influence does not turn on the frequency of social interaction. Instead, the finding that discussant effects on vote choice require neither frequent interaction nor high levels of topic-specific communication is consistent with the structural equivalence model. That is, provided that voters are able to determine the political preferences of their discussants, those preferences may function as cues guiding the voters' own political judgments. This conclusion is similar to that offered by

TABLE 5.5. Political Discussion, Frequency of Discussion, and Electoral Choice

	Presidential	Senate	House
Constant	0.381 (0.728)	0.893** (2.269)	1.021*** (2.681)
Republican	-3.827**** (-9.985)	-2.624**** (-8.067)	-1.826**** (-5.937)
Independent	-1.912**** (-5.035)	-1.397**** (-5.129)	-1.167**** (-4.423)
Ideology	0.389**** (4.111)	0.329**** (5.112)	0.108* (1.832)
IncR	—	—	-1.256**** (-4.071)
Open	—	—	1.434*** (3.059)
Republican x open	—	—	-2.380*** (-3.002)
Pittsburgh	0.186 (0.574)	-1.505**** (-6.195)	0.166 (0.640)
Discussant PID	0.373 (1.361)	0.137 (0.635)	0.250 (1.275)
Frequency of discussion with main discussant	0.441** (2.415)	0.145 (1.066)	-0.209 (-1.651)
Discussant PID x frequency of discussion with main discussant	0.150 (1.154)	-0.009 (-0.091)	0.024 (0.263)
N	453	520	519
Model chi-square	328.337	240.166	182.511

Note: Dependent variables are the two-party vote, coded 1 if respondent voted Democratic, 0 if respondent voted Republican; t-values are in parentheses.
  * $p < .10$, ** $p < .05$, *** $p < .01$, **** $p < .001$

TABLE 5.6. Political Discussion, Topic-Specific Discussion, and Electoral Choice

	Presidential	Senate	House
Constant	1.536** (2.573)	1.172**** (3.375)	1.100*** (3.213)
Republican	-3.771**** (-9.255)	-2.589**** (-8.201)	-1.876**** (-6.173)
Independent	-1.751**** (-4.825)	-1.338**** (-5.020)	-1.167**** (-4.467)
Ideology	0.389**** (4.111)	0.315**** (5.052)	0.093 (1.609)
IncR	—	—	-1.308**** (-4.265)
Open	—	—	1.387*** (2.963)
Republican x open	—	—	-2.194*** (-2.965)
Pittsburgh	0.121 (0.390)	-1.616**** (-6.682)	0.007 (0.028)
Discussant PID	0.222 (0.501)	0.454** (2.250)	0.308** (2.102)
Frequency of discussion about presidential/Senate/ House election	-0.103 (-0.510)	0.065 (0.493)	-0.213* (-1.853)
Discussant PID x frequency of discussion about presidential/Senate/ House election	0.165 (0.996)	-0.175* (-1.784)	-0.002 (-0.029)
N	469	541	535
Model chi-square	326.974	247.830	187.462

Note: Dependent variables are the two-party vote, coded 1 if respondent voted Democratic, 0 if respondent voted Republican; t-values are in parentheses.

* $p < .10$, ** $p < .05$, *** $p < .01$, **** $p < .001$

Huckfeldt and Sprague (1991), who find that discussant effects on the presidential vote choice do not vary in response to the perceived competence of discussants or the intimacy of discussant relationships.

From the perspective of the social equivalence model, discussant effects on vote choice represent the result of a cue-seeking process in which voters turn to their social networks for political signals. Studies of the psychology of cue-based decision making argue that reliance on external cues is most prominent when decision makers lack the motivation or the ability to engage in systematic assessment of relevant data (e.g., Chaiken 1980; Chaiken, Liberman, and Eagly 1989; Mondak 1993c, 1993d). For example, if the decision maker's ability to form a judgment is limited because factual information is unavailable, deference to external cues will be more probable.

From this viewpoint, lack of access to local newspapers may prompt greater reliance by voters on the guiding force of social interaction. In other words, political discussion may be a stronger predictor of the vote in Pittsburgh than in Cleveland. Further, because the newspaper strike reduced overall levels of media exposure only for the House elections, the difference in discussant influence in Cleveland and Pittsburgh should be especially prominent for the House vote.

The logit estimates in table 5.7 yield only weak evidence that media access moderates discussant effects. Initially, note that the influence of discussion on the House vote is nearly twice as great in Pittsburgh as in Cleveland. This effect is consistent with the structural equivalence model, because it appears that cue taking increases when media access is limited. Likewise, discussion effects for the presidential vote are somewhat stronger in Pittsburgh than in Cleveland. For the Senate vote, there is no discussant influence in Pittsburgh, compared with moderate influence in Cleveland. This disparity is interesting when we recall from table 5.3 that voters in Pittsburgh talked about their Senate race to a greater extent than did voters in Cleveland. The absence of discussant influence on the Senate vote in Pittsburgh is strongly inconsistent with the social cohesion model; more talk apparently brought less influence.

Results in table 5.7 suggest that reliance on social cues may hinge, at least to an extent, on the voter's need for those cues. Still, support for the structural equivalence model is less than overwhelming. First, the difference between discussant influence on electoral choice in Pittsburgh and Cleveland falls short of statistical significance for all three sets of elections.[6] Second, as figures 6–8 reveal, the differences between Cleveland and Pittsburgh are substantively minimal. Figure 6 shows that discussion exerts considerable influence on the presidential vote, but that the discussion effect is only slightly greater in Pittsburgh than in Cleveland. Exactly the opposite pattern emerges in figure 7, where discussion produces little influence on the Senate vote in Cleveland, and virtually no effect in Pittsburgh. Finally, in figure 8 we see that discussion produces moderate influence on the House vote in Cleveland, and that the effect of discussion is somewhat greater in magnitude in Pittsburgh.

Collectively, figures 6–8 indicate that Pittsburgh's newspaper strike brought little impact on the tendency of voters to turn to their social networks for electoral cues. In short, it appears that the direct influence of

TABLE 5.7. Political Discussion, Media Access, and Electoral Choice

	Presidential	Senate	House
Constant	1.322*** (3.483)	1.271**** (4.455)	0.802*** (2.822)
Republican	-3.865**** (-9.370)	-2.603**** (-8.311)	-1.931**** (-6.372)
Independent	-1.772**** (-4.879)	-1.341**** (-5.031)	-1.212**** (-4.629)
Ideology	0.352**** (3.948)	0.311**** (4.993)	0.089 (1.550)
IncR	—	—	-1.425**** (-4.520)
Open			1.358*** (2.955)
Republican x open	—	—	-2.163*** (-2.951)
Pittsburgh	0.159 (0.515)	-1.553**** (-6.480)	0.077 (0.304)
Discussant PID, Pittsburgh	0.790**** (4.871)	0.040 (0.367)	0.375**** (3.590)
Discussant PID, Cleveland	0.517*** (3.206)	0.253* (1.960)	0.190 (1.648)
N	471	542	538
Model chi-square	328.210	246.618	188.639

Note: Dependent variables are the two-party vote, coded 1 if respondent voted Democratic, 0 if respondent voted Republican; *t*-values are in parentheses.
  * $p < .10$, ** $p < .05$, *** $p < .01$, **** $p < .001$

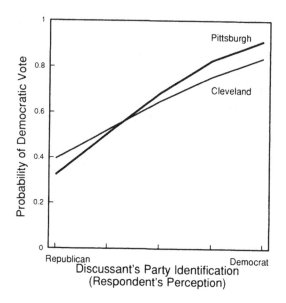

Fig. 6. Political discussion, media access, and the presidential vote. (Data from table 5.7.)

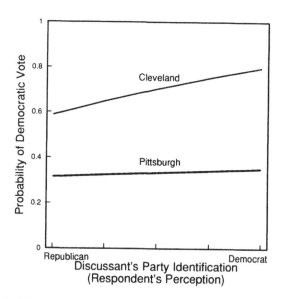

Fig. 7. Political discussion, media access, and the Senate vote. (Data from table 5.7.)

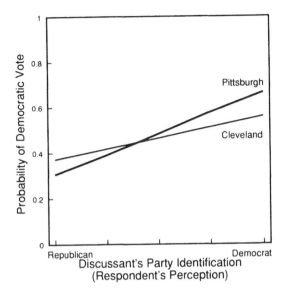

Fig. 8. Political discussion, media access, and the House vote. (Data from table 5.7.)

political discussion on electoral choice is not affected in any substantial manner by the voter's access to news media. In electoral contexts where media exposure is significantly restricted, contexts such as Pittsburgh's House races in 1992, voters may become slightly more reliant on cues received through social interaction. Nonetheless, the effect is so minimal that it suggests that media and discussion essentially do not compete as sources of electoral influence.

Conclusion

When Pittsburgh's newspapers stopped printing, the dynamics of interpersonal political discussion apparently changed only minimally. Those changes that did and did not occur provide evidence pertinent to two significant questions: whether the relationship between news media and political discussion is conflicting or complementary, and what mechanism underlies discussant influence on electoral choice. By speaking to these questions, this chapter also provides additional evidence regarding the electoral significance of local newspapers.

A fundamental question for students of the relationship between news media and social networks is whether these information sources produce conflicting or complementary influence on political behavior.

Findings reported in this chapter demonstrate the existence of a multifaceted relationship. The first issue is *exposure*. The evidence is clear on this point: Pittsburgh's newspaper strike limited voters' exposure to media reports concerning the local U.S. House races, and interpersonal discussion of those elections declined in response. That is, exposure to news media fuels topic-specific discussion, indicating a complementary relationship. News media and interpersonal discussion are neither mutually exclusive nor interchangeable. Instead, media coverage provides some of the subject matter for interpersonal political discourse. For local political affairs, this finding reveals a significant role played by the local newspaper. Because other media generally do not provide thorough coverage of local elections, the quantity of political discussion about those elections largely hinges on the news disseminated by the local papers.

In examining the relationship between media and discussion, the second issue is *influence*. Exposure to information does not assure that the information will affect the recipient's subsequent political behavior. Indeed, on an intuitive level we should expect that as the voter is exposed to more distinct information sources, the influence of any particular source will decline. In other words, the relationship between media and discussion may be complementary when we examine levels of exposure, yet conflicting when we consider the question of influence. However, this chapter's empirical findings constitute less than rousing support for the existence of any form of conflict between news media and discussion. Discussant influence on the vote choice was strong for the media-rich presidential campaign, indicating that access to high levels of campaign news does not inoculate the voter against social influence. In the House races, voters in Pittsburgh endured an extremely media-poor information context, yet discussant influence on the House vote was only marginally more prominent than in Cleveland. The House results suggest the possibility that in extreme cases, where news coverage simply is not available, discussant influence on the vote choice would be especially prominent. But this clearly is an unrealistic extreme in American politics, because no congressional election fully escapes media attention. Thus, while news media and political discussion are complementary information sources, they appear to be essentially unrelated as determinants of electoral choice.

Because interpersonal discussion does influence electoral choice, insight regarding the mechanism underlying that effect contributes to our understanding of political decision making. Two models of decision making have been proposed to account for discussant influence. In this chapter, no support has been provided for the social cohesion model, which holds that discussant influence is the result of explicitly persuasive discourse. Neither the frequency of communication nor the level of campaign-specific discussion have been found to moderate the impact of discussant partisanship on the vote choices of the Cleveland and Pittsburgh respondents. Provided that two people talk, the political predispositions of one may influence the electoral decisions of the other—regardless of how often the two talk, and regardless of whether or not they discuss particular political campaigns.

These results indicate that social influence on political behavior is more broad and more subtle than suggested by the social cohesion model. Hence, findings are consistent with the structural equivalence model, which holds that voters sample their social networks for behavioral cues. It is not the case that persuasive campaigns launched by a few active citizens will sway large numbers of uninformed or apathetic voters. Instead, social influence occurs because most voters cast a wide net when endeavoring to acquire political information. Voters do pay some attention to news reports, debates, and campaign advertisements, but voters also elicit relevant information from everyday life (Popkin 1991; Huckfeldt and Sprague 1991). Political discussion is part of the information mix.

One final point merits attention. We have seen in previous chapters that newspapers seemingly play little unique role in electoral politics. If other media cover a campaign, then the voter gains no special benefit by turning to local newspapers rather than television, magazines, and so on. It is only when newspapers dominate campaign coverage, as in the case of U.S. House elections, that lack of access to a local newspaper meaningfully affects political behavior. This chapter provides additional evidence. Pittsburgh's newspaper strike failed to affect the quantity of political discussion, the frequency of conversation with particular discussion partners, respondents' perceptions of their discussion partners, or topic-specific discussion about the Senate election, the presidential election, or issues. Respondents found alternative media sources, and thus the relationship between media and discussion continued unchanged. The single aspect of discussion relationships affected by the strike was topic-specific discourse focusing on the local U.S. House campaigns. Discussion declined only because media access was constrained, not because newspapers hold an advantage in format over other news mediums. Local newspapers contribute to political discussion because they are the sole source of news about some aspects of the political world.

CHAPTER 6

Electoral Choice

What goes on in your mind?
What goes on in your head?
Who did you think I would be?
Ha! Well you got me instead
—Johnette Napolitano

That this study centers on the 1992 elections indicates an implicit assumption on my part that information matters to voters. Were I of the opinion that the vote choice reflects nothing more than either an individual's long-term political predispositions or random decision-making processes, then I would have expected comparisons of data from Cleveland and Pittsburgh to produce null results at every turn—hardly a motivating proposition! At minimum, it seems obvious that the great wealth of information disseminated by news media over the course of a presidential election must affect voters. When we factor in news reports about subnational elections and interpersonal discussion of politics, support strengthens even further for the intuition that information matters. Hence, the effort to examine the electoral significance of Pittsburgh's newspaper strike was initiated with bold optimism that I would find *something*.

Curiously, however, regardless of how obvious it may seem that the information transmitted over the course of a political campaign will influence electoral decision making, the empirical record is far from persuasive. Beginning with the findings of the Columbia researchers (Lazarsfeld, Berelson, and Gaudet 1944; Berelson, Lazarsfeld, and McPhee 1954), countless studies have reported that news media have only minimal effects in U.S. elections. Voters, such studies suggest, pay little or no attention to information that emerges in the months leading up to an election. Instead, long-term factors such as party identification structure the vote choices of many individuals, whereas other voters cast essentially random ballots.

Although a generation of research has chipped away at the minimal-effects perspective, it nonetheless remains the case that empirical support for the proposition that media matter is less than overwhelming (Bartels 1993). This limitation can be traced, at least in part, to deficiencies in many studies' theoretical frameworks. Much of the literature on the political significance of news media is unabashedly atheoretical, with researchers simply searching for any sign at all that media coverage of an election influences the vote choice. The problem with such a strategy is that information effects may be both subtle and complex, and thus may escape detection when the analyst casts a wide but porous net. Before considering whether or not information matters, we first must determine precisely how and why an individual will likely draw on campaign-specific information when deciding which candidate to support.

Random choice and cautious scrutiny of all available information are not the sole decision-making options available to voters, but rather the two ends of an extensive continuum. A central contribution of research in the field of political cognition is the notion that the citizen who relies on a variety of cognitive efficiency mechanisms when monitoring a political campaign can form a well-grounded decision while ignoring large bodies of relevant information (e.g., Popkin 1991; Sniderman, Brody, and Tetlock 1991; Mondak 1994). From this perspective, the voter desires to balance reliability in decision making with efficiency in information processing. Hence, construction of the vote choice exemplifies the "bounded rationality" described by Simon (1957). Popkin (1991) contends, for instance, that electoral decision making is characterized by "low-information rationality" because the voter elicits cues from the various bits of information he or she receives in everyday life.

If efficiency-minded voters strive to simplify the electoral choice while still basing their votes on meaningful criteria, then news media's campaign coverage may be influential to the extent that it highlights particular cues. Viewed from such a perspective, the newspaper strike enables two empirical tests. First, when the information context suddenly changes, as it did in Pittsburgh in 1992, we can ascertain whether or not the criteria that determine the vote change in response. In short, did access to a major local newspaper enable Cleveland residents to construct vote choices in a manner that Pittsburgh residents could not? If the information structure underlying the vote does not differ in Pittsburgh and Cleveland, it would be difficult to conclude that a person's access to news media meaningfully affects the process of electoral decision making. Second, the adaptive capacity of the voter can be assessed. Does the desire for efficiency mean that the voter passively accepts whatever information happens by, or does the voter actively work to construct a viable information network? Evidence that voters actively work to acquire relevant information would stand in stark contrast to the many studies that portray the American electorate as apathetic and unsophisticated.

The influence of any single type of campaign-specific information should not be considered in isolation. Instead, an obvious starting point is to examine the relationship between the momentary effects of new information and voters' long-term partisan predispositions. The next step will then be to assess the possibility that access to a local newspaper influences which other campaign-specific signals citizens draw on when constructing the vote choice.

Partisanship and Information Acquisition

A voter's long-term partisan attachment is well recognized as one of the strongest determinants of electoral choice. However, the relationship between party identification and campaign-specific information is less clear. Where a partisan identity exists prior to the events of a particular political campaign, what factors determine whether the voter will simply follow the party line or will instead take into account new information that emerges in the weeks and months before the election? Because Pittsburgh's newspaper strike limited the amount of new information some voters received, comparison of the influence of partisanship on the vote in Pittsburgh and in Cleveland may help to reveal how partisan attachments relate to the process of information acquisition.

As a starting point, it is useful to contrast the viewpoint suggested by the Michigan school (e.g., Campbell et al. 1960) with Popkin's (1991) recent discussion of the electoral role of low-information rationality. The Michigan model, of course, places strong emphasis on partisanship as a primary determinant of the vote. From this perspective, voters who possess long-standing partisan attachments vote in accordance with those affiliations, and thus do not respond to the momentary influence of campaign-specific information. Hence, the newspaper strike might have complicated the voting process for persons who lack permanent partisan attachments, but it would have been only a minor inconvenience for those voters who do identify with one of the major parties.

Popkin (1991), drawing on both the work of Downs (1957) and theories from the field of social psychology, argues that the Michigan perspective misrepresents the relationship between partisanship and information acquisition. Operating within the parameters of low-information rationality, voters gather what information they can during a campaign, and then draw on the accumulated data base when constructing the vote choice. In some instances, however, the electoral decision may be too complicated or relevant information may be too scarce. In these cases, Popkin argues, the voter is forced to fall back on partisanship as a default mechanism. Therefore, the preexistence of a partisan attachment should be most important in determining the vote when the information context is least conducive to low-information rationality. Evidence in support of this perspective has emerged from laboratory studies demonstrating that participants tend to fall back on the partisan cue when the decision-making context is relatively complex (Riggle 1992; Riggle et al. 1992).

The newspaper strike offers an opportunity to test the key points of disagreement that distinguish Popkin's theory from the Michigan approach. The strike complicated the process of information acquisition for all elections, and severely constrained the actual amount of information available concerning the local U.S. House campaigns. From the perspective of the Michigan school, these developments should have been largely irrelevant for partisans in the electorate. If partisanship comes before campaign-specific information, then the influence of partisanship on the vote should not differ in Pittsburgh and Cleveland. From Popkin's perspective, in contrast, the strike should be precisely the sort of event that would trigger voters to rely heavily on default mechanisms. In Cleveland, the ready availability of news reports meant that voters did not have to fall back on the simple cue provided by partisanship, but Pittsburgh's voters were not so fortuitous. Hence, evidence that partisan attachments more strongly influenced the vote in Pittsburgh than in Cleveland would support the thesis that partisanship serves as a default mechanism.

The importance of the partisan affiliation as a determinant of the vote may vary as a function of the strength of the attachment. We know that weak partisans defect in support of the opposing party's candidates at much higher rates than do strong partisans (e.g., Flanigan and Zingale 1991). This point suggests that strong partisans may be relatively impervious to the influence of temporal forces, but that weak partisans may draw heavily on available campaign-specific information. This distinction potentially provides an opportunity to reconcile the perspectives offered by Popkin and the Michigan analysts. That is, partisanship may be a nearly all-powerful determinant of the vote only for strong partisans, whereas weak partisans may view the partisan identity more as a fallback position to be used only when the review of more immediate information is inconclusive.

To assess the relationship between partisanship and information acquisition, data will be examined for the presidential, Senate, and House elections. The possibility that the influence of partisanship varies for strong and weak partisans will be considered through the estimation of separate statistical models for those respondents who do and do not hold strong partisan attachments.

The Presidential Vote

If partisanship provides the voter with a default judgment, then the influence of party identification on the presidential vote should be greatest where the information context is the most anemic. In other words, the voter who lacks access to campaign-specific information may have to fall back on the guiding force of partisanship. Hence, if the presidential vote in Pittsburgh followed party lines more so than in Cleveland, we could conclude that the newspaper strike drove Pittsburgh voters to rely on partisanship as a default mechanism. Conversely, an absence of variance between the two regions would suggest that partisanship is a stable source of influence on the vote, and one that operates prior to any temporal factors.

Two statistical models will be estimated, one including self-identified strong partisans and one including weak partisans and independents. If a sparse information context elaborates the influence of partisanship on the vote, that effect should be the most prominent among weak partisans, persons for whom party identification is not normally at the forefront of political decision making. Strong partisans, in contrast, may be relatively insulated against the effects of campaign-specific information. Therefore, if partisanship exerts greater influence on the presidential vote in Pittsburgh than in Cleveland, the difference between the two regions may peak for weak partisans.

The logit estimates reported in table 6.1 show partisanship to be equally influential as a determinant of the presidential vote in Cleveland and in Pittsburgh.[1] As in chapter 5, "Republican" is a dummy variable isolating self-identified Republicans. This variable yields negative coefficients because self-identified Republicans are relatively unlikely to vote for a Democratic presidential candidate. Had Pittsburgh voters been forced to fall back on the partisan cue, the Pittsburgh × Republican interaction terms would have produced statistically significant *negative* coefficients, indicating an elaboration of the effects of partisanship. Instead, for both strong and weak partisans, we see insignificant positive coefficients. Hence, the results seem much more consistent with the process described by the Michigan school than with Popkin's contention that partisanship functions as a default mechanism.

A case could be made that the presidential race is an inappropriate context in which to contrast the Michigan and Popkin theories. In previous chapters, we have seen little evidence that the Pittsburgh strike prevented voters from acquiring information pertaining to the 1992 presidential election. The strike may have complicated matters a bit, but voters who were unable to receive information from a local newspaper succeeded in locating acceptable substitutes. Consequently, voters in Pittsburgh equaled their Cleveland counterparts in knowledge about the presidential campaign, and patterns of interpersonal political discussion in the two cities were quite similar. Cumulatively, the evidence concerning the presidential election suggests that Pittsburgh voters adapted well to the strike. Rather than passively accepting their fates as victims of a sparse information context, the voters actively constructed functional information networks. Therefore, the results in table 6.1 leave open the possibility that partisanship acts as a default mechanism. That is, the null results in table 6.1 may indicate that Pittsburgh's presidential voters had no *need* to rely on a fallback position due to their success in finding alternative information sources.

Comparison of the two logit models in table 6.1 reveals very different patterns of voting behavior for strong and weak partisans. Not surprisingly, the direction of a person's partisan affiliation matters much more for strong than for weak partisans, as indicated by the

TABLE 6.1. The Strength of Partisan Attachments and the Influence of Partisanship on the Presidential Vote

	Strong Partisans	Weak Partisans and Independents
Constant	3.766***	0.569
	(3.244)	(1.347)
Republican	-6.841****	-2.997****
	(-5.444)	(-4.502)
Independent	—	-1.024***
		(-2.694)
Ideology	0.187	0.368****
	(0.946)	(3.684)
Pittsburgh	-0.788	0.172
	(-0.636)	(0.469)
Pittsburgh x Republican	0.372	0.742
	(0.230)	(0.918)
N	247	226
Model chi-square	257.247	65.283

Note: Dependent variable is the two-party vote, coded 1 if respondent voted Democratic, 0 if respondent voted Republican; *t*-values are in parentheses.
* $p < .10$, ** $p < .05$, *** $p < .01$, **** $p < .001$

extremely large coefficient for the Republican dummy variable in column one. Conversely, ideology adds structure to the vote only for weak partisans and independents. The model chi-square statistics are also revealing. Although the model chi-square is not a true goodness-of-fit measure, the difference between the two scores is far from subtle. The statistic for column one indicates that for strong partisans, partisanship fully structures the vote choice. Indeed, a mere 3 percent of this study's self-identified strong partisans defected in support of the opposing party's presidential nominee. With such overwhelming party-line voting as the norm among strong partisans, it appears that no room existed for the newspaper strike to magnify the influence of partisanship. Therefore, at least for strong partisans, it seems improbable that the quality of the information context will alter the structure of electoral choice.

The Senate Vote

Thus far, analysis of data concerning the Pennsylvania and Ohio Senate campaigns has produced results resembling those for the presidential election in that the absence of local newspapers did not hamper information acquisition among Pittsburgh-area voters. Broadcast media and national print sources provided coverage of the Pennsylvania Senate election sufficient to enable Pittsburgh voters to overcome the lack of a local newspaper. As a result, the only Cleveland versus Pittsburgh differences detected in earlier chapters apparently stem from the unique features of the two Senate campaigns, rather than from variance in the quantity or quality of information available to Senate voters in the two regions. In light of the high salience of the Pennsylvania Senate race, and given that Pittsburgh voters found alternative information sources to replace their missing newspapers, it is unlikely that reliance on partisanship as a default mechanism will be more common in Pittsburgh than in Cleveland.

The logit estimates shown in table 6.2 reveal a significant interaction between partisanship and region for both strong and weak partisans—Senate voters in Pittsburgh were *less* likely to vote in accordance with their own partisan affiliations than were Senate voters in Cleveland, a pattern precisely the opposite of what we would expect if partisanship served as a default judgment in Pittsburgh. The strike not only failed to compel reliance on partisanship as a default mechanism, but Pittsburgh voters apparently received enough campaign-specific information to enable rather free defection from the party line. That such defection was more common in Pittsburgh than in Cleveland likely reflects Republican

Arlen Specter's ability to garner support from Democrats due to his image as an ideological moderate. Additionally, challenger Lynn Yeakel's "Year of the Woman" campaign, with its roots in the Anita Hill-Clarence Thomas controversy, crossed conventional partisan divisions. In contrast, Ohio's Glenn-DeWine Senate election was relatively standard political fare, and thus it is not surprising that many Cleveland respondents voted the party line.

Moving beyond the question of campaign-specific variance in this study's two Senate elections, the important point to emerge from table 6.2 is that the influence of partisanship on the Senate vote was not greater in Pittsburgh than in Cleveland. As with results for the presidential election, it again appears that where voters are able to construct functional information networks, reliance on partisanship as a default mechanism does not occur.

TABLE 6.2. The Strength of Partisan Attachments and the Influence of Partisanship on the Senate Vote

	Strong Partisans	Weak Partisans and Independents
Constant	3.585**** (3.435)	0.981*** (2.670)
Republican	-5.845**** (-5.207)	-2.596**** (-4.841)
Independent	—	-0.965*** (-3.039)
Ideology	0.265** (2.524)	0.330**** (4.053)
Pittsburgh	-3.492*** (-3.341)	-1.792**** (-5.516)
Pittsburgh x Republican	2.743** (2.163)	1.539** (2.311)
N	256	290
Model chi-square	190.527	82.124

Note: Dependent variable is the two-party vote, coded 1 if respondent voted Democratic, 0 if respondent voted Republican; t-values are in parentheses.
* $p < .10$, ** $p < .05$, *** $p < .01$, **** $p < .001$

The House Vote

Pittsburgh's newspaper strike limited the actual amount of information voters received about their respective U.S. House elections. Because the voters were unable to find acceptable alternative information sources, the voters admitted to holding relatively low levels of knowledge about the local House campaigns. Consequently, the House elections enable a more direct test of the role of partisanship than did the presidential and Senate campaigns. If partisanship functions as a default mechanism, comparison of Pittsburgh and Cleveland data should reveal that Pittsburgh's information-starved House voters closely followed the party line.

The logit estimates depicted in table 6.3 provide no support for the thesis that partisanship functions as a fallback position for those voters for whom campaign-specific information does not abound. Despite the existence of a rather sparse information context, Pittsburgh House voters were no more likely to base their votes on partisan affiliations than were voters in Cleveland. Indeed, the only magnification of partisan effects suggested in table 6.3 is for voters in Ohio's Nineteenth District, an open seat, where the absence of incumbency as a cue appears to have slightly intensified the inclination of strong partisans to vote in accordance with their partisan attachments.

The absence of uniquely strong partisan effects among Pittsburgh's House voters raises two questions. First, if partisanship is not a default mechanism, what role does it play in structuring the vote? Popkin's (1991) contention that partisan attachments provide fallback judgments for efficiency-minded voters has received no support here. Instead, this study's results coincide better with the perspective suggested by the Michigan school; partisanship is an underlying predisposition that inclines the voter to look more favorably on some candidates than others. The influence of partisanship on the vote varies as a function of the strength of the partisan attachment, and perhaps in response to the particular features of a campaign, but the amount of campaign-specific information available apparently does not moderate the partisanship effect. For self-identified strong partisans, partisanship powerfully determines the vote, to the near exclusion of alternative factors.[2] Weak partisans consider more than just the candidates' partisan affiliations, but the influence of partisanship still does not intensify when the information context is media-poor.

A second question suggested by results for the House elections is if the absence of newspapers brought *any* effect for the structure of electoral choice in Pittsburgh. We know that Pittsburgh's House voters suffered an information gap compared with voters in Cleveland. When constructing the vote, how did Pittsburgh voters adapt to this relative dearth of information? Further, if voters devised new decision-making strategies in response to the newspaper strike, were different approaches taken by strong and weak partisans? To pursue these questions, we must consider what short-term cues Pittsburgh's voters may have used to structure the vote choice in the 1992 House elections.

TABLE 6.3. The Strength of Partisan Attachments and the Influence of Partisanship on the U.S. House Vote

	Strong Partisans	Weak Partisans and Independents
Constant	1.103**	0.721*
	(2.448)	(1.941)
Republican	-2.880****	-2.081****
	(-3.931)	(-3.448)
Independent	—	-1.053****
		(-3.465)
Ideology	0.105	0.122
	(1.188)	(1.618)
IncR	-1.478***	-1.156***
	(-2.957)	(-3.004)
Open	1.816*	0.692
	(1.691)	(1.410)
Republican x open	-2.984*	-0.902
	(-1.844)	(-0.935)
Pittsburgh	0.045	-0.080
	(0.087)	(-0.230)
Pittsburgh x Republican	-0.315	0.811
	(-0.035)	(1.138)
N	255	288
Model chi-square	132.066	50.510

Note: Dependent variable is the two-party vote, coded 1 if respondent voted Democratic, 0 if respondent voted Republican; t-values are in parentheses.
* $p < .10$, ** $p < .05$, *** $p < .01$, **** $p < .001$

News, Cues, and Electoral Choice

At this point, the presidential and Senate campaigns will be abandoned so that greater attention may be given to this study's House elections. Partisanship and political discussion have not been found to influence the presidential and Senate votes more in Pittsburgh than in Cleveland, suggesting that continuing the search for regional variance in voting behavior will be fruitless for all but the House contests. Pittsburgh's House voters suffered an information deficit in 1992, yet did not fall back on partisanship when casting their votes. If a weakened information context does not compel heightened reliance on long-term cues such as the voter's own partisan attachment, then the voter may instead search for election-specific signals. Chapter 5 presented evidence in support of this perspective, with the finding that political discussion was a stronger determinant of the House vote in Pittsburgh than in Cleveland, although the difference between the two regions was only moderate in magnitude. What remains in question is whether that discussion effect varies for strong and weak partisans, and whether other short-term factors also distinguish electoral decision making in media-rich and media-poor information contexts.

In addition to drawing on the guiding force of political discussion, efficiency-minded House voters also may use their own presidential vote choices to inform the subnational decision. The coattail voter connects the presidential and House votes, and thus simplifies the latter choice. Hence, coattail voting may be most prevalent as an efficiency mechanism when voters lack access to relevant campaign-specific information about their local House elections. To explore this point, the relative influence of political discussion and coattail voting will be examined, with particular attention given to the possibility of Cleveland versus Pittsburgh differences in the two effects, and also to possible differences among strong and weak partisans.

Coattail voting is most prominent among voters who lack sensitivity to local political affairs (Mondak 1990), voters with low levels of education (Mondak and McCurley 1994), and voters in open-seat elections (Mondak 1993b; Mondak and McCurley 1994). Each of these effects suggest that the coattail vote is the outcome of a simplifying process in which a person who is unable or unwilling to engage in careful scrutiny of the House candidates simply draws on his or her own presidential vote as a guide. However, despite its efficiency, coattail voting apparently does entail a level of analysis on the part of the voter. Specifically, the more strongly a person prefers one presidential nominee to the other, the stronger the impact of the presidential vote on the House vote

(Mondak and McCurley 1994). Further, the presidential-to-House link peaks when the voter most fully supports the issue positions of the preferred presidential candidate (Mondak 1990). In other words, citizens do not crudely or thoughtlessly extend the presidential vote to lower races. Coattail voting may simplify decision making in House elections, but voters apparently are most likely to turn to this efficiency mechanism if they can connect specific substantive dimensions of the presidential campaign with their local House contests.

The impact of both presidential coattails and interpersonal political discussion should be greater for weak partisans and independents than for strong partisans. We have already seen that the vote choices of strong partisans are overwhelmingly structured by partisanship, presumably leaving little room for the election-specific influence of coattails and discussion. Additionally, the partisan link brought by coattail voting is superfluous for individuals who are predisposed to vote for only one party's candidates. Thus, where a strong partisan attachment is in place prior to an electoral campaign, the voter will be relatively immune to the more temporal effects of presidential coattails, political discussion, and the election reports offered by local news media.

Long-term partisan forces are minimal for self-identified weak partisans and independents. Therefore, such voters should show considerable susceptibility to campaign-specific information. Generally, coattail voting should be common for this group of voters, because the coattail vote provides a means other than sheer partisanship for the individual to connect multiple elections. Unfortunately, it is not so clear whether coattail voting should be expected to be more prevalent in Cleveland or in Pittsburgh. Due to the absence of their local newspapers, Pittsburgh's House voters surely had considerable need for an efficiency mechanism. However, if coattail voting presupposes that the voter can link a presidential nominee's issue agenda with the party's House candidate (Mondak 1990), then the newspaper strike may have undermined the very information base on which coattail voting rests. In short, Pittsburgh voters apparently needed the sort of efficiency associated with coattail voting, yet may have lacked the capacity to construct meaningful links between the presidential and congressional votes.

The uniquely strong reliance of Pittsburgh's House voters on signals transmitted through political discussion was established in chapter 5. In reconsidering that effect here, an obvious expectation is that political discussion will be most influential in Pittsburgh for those voters who are self-identified weak partisans and independents. Such voters are receptive to campaign-specific information, and thus if news media do not provide a sufficient information base, then these voters likely will turn to their social contexts for alternative cues.

Strong Partisans

The modeling strategy I will employ will be to first examine the influence of the presidential vote and political discussion on the House vote, and then to determine whether those effects differ in Cleveland and Pittsburgh. The presidential vote variable is coded 1 (Clinton), 0 (Perot), and -1 (Bush). The initial model in table 6.4 reports the baseline effects, while the second model distinguishes those effects by region. In column one, we see no evidence of coattail voting among strong partisans. Where partisanship already implicitly links the presidential and House campaigns, an individual's own presidential vote is not needed to direct the corresponding House vote. In contrast with expectations, baseline results suggest that political discussion may bring at least marginal influence on the House votes of strong partisans. Still, the effect is slight, and it is dwarfed in magnitude by the influence of partisanship.

Turning to table 6.4's second model, we see that model performance is not improved when variables are added to capture possible Cleveland versus Pittsburgh differences, and that neither the presidential vote nor political discussion exert differential influence in the two regions. The information gap reported by Pittsburgh's House voters apparently was irrelevant for strong partisans, persons for whom long-term political attachments provide insulation against more momentary features of the electoral context. Likewise, coattails also were nonexistent in Ohio's Nineteenth District, even though coattail voting previously has been found to be especially prominent in open seats (Mondak 1993b; Mondak and McCurley 1994). A strong partisan affiliation seemingly precludes the existence of presidential coattails, and allows only minimal influence from interpersonal political discussion.

Weak Partisans and Independents

Although the voting behavior of weak partisans and independents is expected to differ from that of strong partisans, the initial model in table 6.5 leaves considerable ambiguity regarding the nature of those differences. First, coattail voting appears to have occurred only in the study's one open-seat district. Although coattail voting was expected to be more prevalent among weak partisans and independents than among strong partisans, the absence of such a broad-based effect in the first model in table 6.5 matches the finding reported for strong

TABLE 6.4. Strong Partisans: Political Discussion, Presidential Coattails, and the House Vote

	Baseline	Cleveland vs. Pittsburgh
Constant	0.556	0.662
	(1.000)	(1.043)
Republican	-1.724**	-1.770**
	(-2.168)	(-2.117)
Ideology	0.074	0.073
	(0.795)	(0.781)
IncR	-1.387****	-1.514****
	(-3.272)	(-2.912)
Open	1.523	1.304
	(1.150)	(0.952)
Republican x open	-2.440	-2.217
	(-1.183)	(-1.061)
Presidential vote	0.482	0.122
	(1.166)	(0.215)
Discussant PID	0.241*	0.422**
	(1.907)	(1.978)
Presidential vote x open	0.494	0.854
	(0.414)	(0.672)
Pittsburgh	—	-0.033
		(-0.068)
Pittsburgh x discussant PID	—	-0.275
		(-1.040)
Pittsburgh x Presidential vote	—	0.527
		(1.005)
N	249	249
Model chi-square	134.344	135.901

Note: Dependent variable is the two-party vote, coded 1 if respondent voted Democratic, 0 if respondent voted Republican; *t*-values are in parentheses.
 * $p < .10$, ** $p < .05$, *** $p < .01$, **** $p < .001$

TABLE 6.5. Weak Partisans and Independents: Political Discussion, Presidential
Coattails, and the House Vote

	Baseline	Cleveland vs. Pittsburgh
Constant	0.625* (1.801)	0.645* (1.644)
Republican	-1.230*** (-2.993)	-1.282*** (-3.006)
Independent	-0.908*** (-2.821)	-1.048*** (-3.131)
Ideology	0.060 (0.731)	0.035 (0.418)
IncR	-1.220**** (-3.308)	-1.647**** (-3.702)
Open	1.371** (2.053)	1.546** (2.208)
Republican x open	-1.640 (-1.566)	-1.883* (-1.790)
Presidential vote	0.258 (1.166)	0.707** (2.162)
Discussant PID	0.194* (1.680)	-0.174 (-0.989)
Presidential vote x open	1.311** (2.192)	1.076* (1.661)
Pittsburgh	—	0.398 (1.162)
Pittsburgh x discussant PID	—	0.776*** (3.062)
Pittsburgh x presidential vote	—	-0.860** (-2.076)
N	275	275
Model chi-square	67.180	78.788

Note: Dependent variable is the two-party vote, coded 1 if respondent voted Democratic, 0
if respondent voted Republican; t-values are in parentheses.
 * p < .10, ** p < .05, *** p < .01, **** p < .001

partisans in table 6.4. Second, political discussion brings moderate influence on the vote, but the effect is not stronger for weak partisans and
independents than for strong partisans. Figure 9 reveals that the substantive impact of discussion is minimal, as demonstrated by the slight upward slope of the lines across discussant partisanship.[3] The gap between
the two lines in figure 9 suggests a small coattail effect, although the
coefficient for the presidential vote variable falls well short of statistical
significance.

Moving to the second model in table 6.5, first note that model
performance is improved when we take into account variance by region
in discussion effects and coattail voting; the improvement in the model
chi-square versus the baseline model is 11.608 ($p < .05$, 3 df). The
interaction terms have produced an interesting pattern of results: political discussion affects the vote only in Pittsburgh, whereas presidential
coattails matter only in Cleveland. The first of these effects is consistent
with expectations. Some among Pittsburgh's House voters searched
their social contexts for electoral cues due to the information gap caused
by the absence of the city's major newspapers. Hence, the discussion
effect identified in chapter 5 has been refined here with the finding that

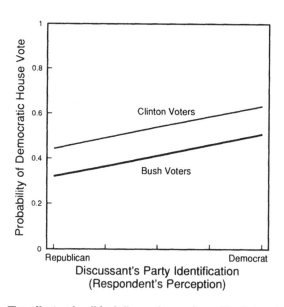

**Fig. 9. The effects of political discussion and presidential coattails on
the House votes of self-identified independents. (Data from table 6.5,
column 1.)**

only Pittsburgh's weak partisans and independents turned to political discussion as a substitute information source.

The strong coattail effect among Cleveland voters indicates that coattail voting did occur in 1992. However, despite their apparent need for external cues, Pittsburgh residents failed to link their presidential and House votes. Lacking access to local newspapers, Pittsburgh voters apparently were unable to draw the substantive, issue-based connection previously found to underlie the coattail vote (Mondak 1990; Mondak and McCurley 1994). Hence, current findings support the premise that coattail voting is a relatively sophisticated rather than coarse decision-making strategy. Coattail voting represents an election-specific link among a party's candidates as perceived by voters who are not themselves strong partisans. It is not enough for two candidates to share the party label. Instead, coattail voting only occurs when the voter receives information sufficient to establish a more tangible connection between a party's presidential and House nominees.

Figure 10 depicts regional variance in the influence of presidential coattails and interpersonal political discussion. In Cleveland (fig. 10A), the large gap between the two lines represents the impact of coattail voting, whereas the absence of an upward slope across discussant partisanship indicates that political discussion did not influence the House vote. Precisely the opposite pattern of results exists in Pittsburgh (fig. 10B), where presidential coattails were absent, but where House voters drew heavily on the signals transmitted through political discussion.

For weak partisans and independents, access to a local newspaper is a critical determinant of the processes they invoke when deciding which House candidates to support. At first glance, it might seem to be a positive thing that Pittsburgh's House voters relied so heavily on political discussion as a replacement for their missing newspapers. After all, discourse and deliberation within the electorate surely must be to the good. However, recall from chapter 5 that the extent to which Pittsburgh respondents actually discussed their House elections declined due to the newspaper strike. Newspapers enable more informed and more frequent discussion. When Pittsburgh voters discussed politics, they did not talk about their House elections because the newspaper strike denied them the raw material necessary for such topic-specific discourse. Consequently, the influence of political discussion on the House vote in Pittsburgh reveals an electorate forced to grasp for any available cue within a rather sparse information environment.

The absence of coattail voting in Pittsburgh further demonstrates the significance of the local newspaper. Coattail voting occurs when the voter can meaningfully connect national and subnational campaigns.

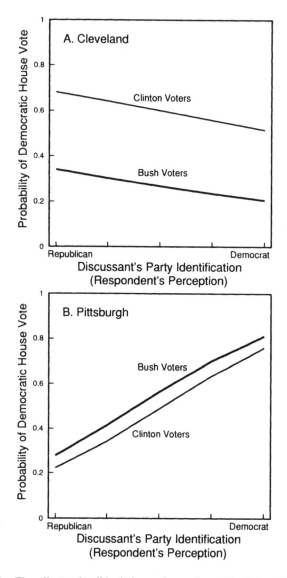

Fig. 10. The effects of political discussion and presidential coattails on the House votes of self-identified independents in Cleveland and Pittsburgh. (Data from table 6.5, column 1.)

The presidential and House votes will not be linked if the voter does not perceive a substantive, and preferably issue-based, relationship between a party's presidential and House candidates. That Pittsburgh voters were unable to see such a connection in 1992 suggests that the local newspaper plays a crucial role in enabling the citizen to appreciate the local importance of national politics. Pittsburgh voters knew what issues were being discussed in the presidential campaign, yet they could not relate that discussion to their own local House elections. The political world thus may seem distant and highly abstract if the citizen is denied local perspective.

The effects depicted in table 6.5 and in figure 10 represent three-way interactions among independent variables: political discussion affects the vote, but primarily for weak partisans and independents living in a media-poor information context; similarly, presidential coattails also affect the vote only for weak partisans and independents, but for persons residing in a media-rich information context. One naturally approaches complex interactive effects such as these with caution. More specifically, it is fair to ask whether the findings are the unique products of this study's highly specialized research context. Although the results hold considerable intuitive appeal, confidence in their generalizability surely would grow if it could be demonstrated that the fundamental pattern of results is not limited in place and time. Unfortunately, a precise replication would require the timely occurrence of a second newspaper strike. While we wait, a more immediate alternative is to elicit general hypotheses from the Cleveland-Pittsburgh findings, and then to test those hypotheses using data from a different electoral context.

A Replication

The initial question in searching for a generalizable pattern of results centers on possible differences in the decision-making processes of strong partisans versus weak partisans and independents. Results to this point support the premise that strong partisans are less susceptible to influence from election-specific information than are voters who lack such well-developed partisan attachments. First, although marginal effects of political discussion were found for strong partisans, a much more powerful discussion effect existed among weak partisans and independents in Pittsburgh. Second, presidential coattails directed the House votes of weak partisans and independents in Cleveland, but had no impact on the electoral choices of strong partisans. If strong partisans commonly cast votes unaffected by temporal forces, then supporting evidence should be widely available. However, the search for effects associated with political discussion and presidential coattails severely constrains the choice among secondary data sets. Data must be available concerning both the presidential and the House campaigns, and the survey also must examine respondents' patterns of interpersonal political discussion.

The 1984 South Bend Study provides data well-suited for a reexamination of the influence of presidential coattails and political discussion on the House vote.[4] The three-wave panel study drew data from 16 neighborhoods in the South Bend, Indiana area, the site of Indiana's Third Congressional District. The third wave of the South Bend Study was conducted after the 1984 elections, and thus resembles the Cleveland-Pittsburgh survey in terms of procedure. Because data are available about both the House and the presidential campaigns, it will be possible to explore the influence of coattail voting among the South Bend respondents. More importantly, the study's third wave includes an extensive battery of questions concerning political discussion. Indeed, the discussion items used on the Cleveland-Pittsburgh survey were deliberately modeled on the South Bend questions, meaning that the discussant partisanship variable created in chapter 5 can be replicated precisely for the South Bend respondents.

What is lacking with the South Bend data, of course, is quasi-experimental manipulation of the information context. In Pittsburgh in 1992, voters were *involuntarily* denied access to their major local newspapers, providing this study's methodological focal point. With the South Bend data, variance in media exposure can be captured only via respondents' self-reports, and any variance that does exist would reflect the *voluntary* information-acquisition patterns of those respondents. On the South Bend Study's post-election wave, respondents were asked how often they read the local newspaper, the *South Bend Tribune*. Results are coded 1 (every day) to 5 (never). If exposure to a local newspaper truly determines the process by which a person constructs the House vote, then the influence of political discussion and presidential coattails may vary in South Bend as a function of how often respondents read the *Tribune*. Such self-report data must be used cautiously, as there are no guarantees that those respondents who received the paper daily either read it closely, or even paid any attention at all to stories concerning the local congressional election. Still, if exposure to a local newspaper serves as a necessary prerequisite for certain types of decision-making processes, then the South Bend Study's self-report item is sufficient to enable a coarse replication of the Cleveland-Pittsburgh analyses.

The unique features of the House race in Indiana's Third District must be taken into account. In 1984, the incumbent was Republican

John Hiler. Hiler won reelection in 1984, although Democratic challenger Michael Barnes captured the South Bend area. Hiler came to office in 1980 with a surprising upset of a 22-year veteran, John Brademas. In both 1980 and 1984, Hiler strongly emphasized his support for Ronald Reagan, and thus likely magnified the influence of coattail voting. Consequently, we should expect to find a coattail effect when examining the South Bend data, and it is possible that the magnitude of that effect will be considerable.

Beginning with strong partisans, results in table 6.6 closely resemble the Cleveland-Pittsburgh findings seen earlier. First, partisanship

TABLE 6.6. Strong Partisans and the 1984 House Vote in South Bend, Indiana

	Baseline	Media Exposure
Constant	1.637**	2.087**
	(2.050)	(2.158)
Republican	-4.425****	-4.614****
	(-5.090)	(-5.052)
Ideology	0.168	0.160
	(1.238)	(1.120)
Presidential vote	0.576	0.121
	(0.664)	(0.093)
Discussant PID	0.113	-0.324
	(0.670)	(-0.970)
Exposure to local print media	—	-0.263
		(-0.646)
Exposure to local print media x presidential vote	—	0.374
		(0.531)
Exposure to local print media x discussant PID	—	0.308
		(1.591)
N	322	322
Model chi-square	303.845	307.200

Source: Data from 1984 South Bend Study.

Note: Dependent variable is the two-party vote, coded 1 if respondent voted Democratic, 0 if respondent voted Republican; *t*-values are in parentheses.

* $p < .10$, ** $p < .05$, *** $p < .01$, **** $p < .001$

functions as an extremely crisp determinant of the House vote.[5] Even more so than in Cleveland or Pittsburgh, South Bend voters appear to have walked the party line. Second, neither the presidential vote (coded 1 if respondent voted for Mondale, 0 if Reagan) nor political discussion[6] influence the vote choices of strong partisans. Third, estimates for the second model in table 6.6 reveal that exposure to the local newspaper, the *South Bend Tribune*, did not moderate the susceptibility of strong partisans to campaign-specific signals. Once again we see that the preexistence of a strong partisan affiliation insulates the voter from the effects of presidential coattails, political discussion, and the news coverage of local print media.

Unlike strong partisans, weak partisans and independents cast votes presumably structured by factors other than blanket partisan attachments. Consequently, alternative signals such as the respondent's own presidential vote may matter the most as determinants of the House vote among weak partisans and independents. Evidence in support of this thesis emerged from the Cleveland data analyzed in table 6.5, and further corroboration is shown in the initial model in table 6.7. The coefficient for the Republican dummy variable is only one-third as large for South Bend's weak partisans as for the area's strong partisans, demonstrating that partisan effects drop quickly when the partisan attachment weakens. However, this gap in the structure underlying the House vote is fully replaced by the influence of presidential coattails, as indicated by the rather large coefficient for the presidential vote dummy variable in table 6.7. In both Cleveland and in South Bend, we have seen that presidential coattails matter only for weak partisans and independents. The presidential vote can provide an election-specific connection between a party's candidates, but that linkage is superfluous for strong partisans.

Political discussion affected the House votes of Pittsburgh's weak partisans and independents, but failed to exert comparable influence in Cleveland. That differential effect suggests that voters look to their social environments for electoral signals when the information context is media-poor. The baseline model in table 6.7 provides support for this perspective. Although discussion does strongly influence the House vote in South Bend, the coefficient for the discussant partisanship variable is less than half as large as the effect for Pittsburgh voters reported in table 6.5. It may not take a newspaper strike for discussion to inform the House vote, but a weakened media context clearly seems to elaborate the discussion effect. In figure 11, the slight upward slope of the two lines represents the influence of discussant partisanship, an effect that is visibly overwhelmed by presidential coattails.

Turning to the second model in table 6.7, note initially that political discussion does not grow in influence for those weak partisans and independents who lack regular exposure to the local newspaper. This effect is nominally inconsistent with the Pittsburgh results, given that political discussion contributed greatly to the House votes of Pittsburgh's weak partisans and independents. Lacking access to a local newspaper, Pittsburgh voters actively searched their social environments for electoral

TABLE 6.7. Weak Partisans, Independents, and the 1984 House Vote in South Bend, Indiana

	Baseline	Media Exposure
Constant	-0.396** (-2.143)	-0.343 (-1.173)
Republican	-1.472**** (-4.248)	-1.452**** (-4.207)
Independent	-0.497** (-2.050)	-0.519** (-2.130)
Ideology	0.105* (1.671)	0.102 (1.612)
Presidential vote	3.102**** (9.852)	4.035**** (6.773)
Discussant PID	0.263**** (3.495)	0.249* (1.696)
Exposure to local print media	—	-0.026 (-0.176)
Exposure to local print media x presidential vote	—	-0.581** (-1.962)
Exposure to local print media x discussant PID	—	0.010 (0.113)
N	670	670
Model chi-square	363.576	369.448

Source: Data from 1984 South Bend Study.
Note: Dependent variable is the two-party vote, coded 1 if respondent voted Democratic, 0 if respondent voted Republican; *t*-values are in parentheses.
 * $p < .10$, ** $p < .05$, *** $p < .01$, **** $p < .001$

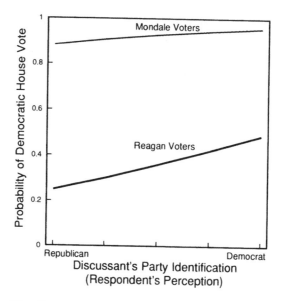

Fig. 11. The effects of political discussion and presidential coattails on the House votes of self-identified independents in South Bend, Indiana, 1984. (Data from table 6.7, column 1.)

signals, yet comparable behavior apparently did not occur among those South Bend voters who declined to read the local newspaper. The most plausible explanation for the difference in results for Pittsburgh and South Bend is that lack of exposure to local newspapers was involuntary in Pittsburgh, but voluntary in South Bend. Pittsburgh voters had an information source taken away, and thus endeavored to locate an acceptable alternative. In contrast, some South Bend voters voluntarily chose to minimize their exposure to political information. It is quite reasonable that interpersonal discussion is not uniquely influential for such voters.[7]

Results from the Cleveland-Pittsburgh data support the conclusion that coattail voting presupposes that the voter has received information sufficient to link substantive elements of a party's presidential and congressional candidacies. If media exposure is a prerequisite for coattail voting, then the absence of exposure to one's local newspaper should weaken the effect of the presidential vote on the corresponding House vote regardless of whether that absence of exposure is voluntary or involuntary. South Bend results bolster this contention, as indicated by the presidential vote variables in the second model in table 6.7. In figure 12, we see that the gap between Mondale and Reagan voters closes by

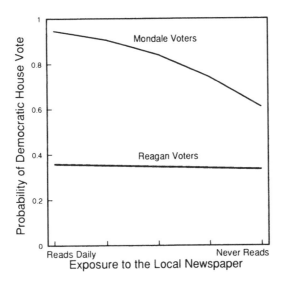

Fig. 12. Exposure to local print media and the effect of presidential coattails on the House votes of self-identified independents in South Bend, Indiana, 1984. (Data from table 6.7, column 2.)

over half as exposure to the *South Bend Tribune* declines. Voters who, for whatever reason, do not read a local newspaper are relatively unlikely to use their presidential votes to direct the corresponding choice among House candidates.

The impact of media exposure on coattail voting appears to have influenced only South Bend's Mondale voters. If the lack of exposure to a local newspaper weakens the presidential-to-House connection, why was coattail voting among South Bend's Reagan voters unaffected? Two reasons are apparent. First, Republican incumbent John Hiler actively depicted himself as a Reagan supporter, drawing a clear link between the two candidates. Hence, Reagan voters were not uniquely reliant on the local newspaper for information connecting the Reagan and Hiler campaigns. Second, unlike any campaign in the Cleveland-Pittsburgh data set, Hiler and Reagan also had been partisan running mates four years previously, when both first gained office in 1980. Once in Congress, Hiler earned a reputation as one of the House's "Reagan Robots." Given that the two incumbents had served so closely together in Washington for four years, even the most isolated of voters could glean some evidence of a relationship between the two Republicans.

Examination of the South Bend data has produced evidence in support of the fundamental conclusions suggested by patterns of voting

behavior in Cleveland and Pittsburgh. First, weak partisans and independents are more susceptible to campaign-specific signals than are strong
partisans. Second, coattail voting matters exclusively for weak partisans
and independents. Third, exposure to local print media helps the voter
to connect the presidential and House campaigns, and thus increases the
prevalence of coattail voting. Fourth, voters whose access to relevant
news media is involuntarily constrained (Pittsburgh) are more reliant on
political discussion as a determinant of the House vote than are voters
whose access to new media continues uninterrupted (Cleveland, South
Bend). Collectively, these results portray voters who work actively yet
flexibly to acquire electoral information.

Conclusion

When studying electoral choice, political scientists often have focused
on voters' long-term political predispositions at the expense of attention
to the dynamics of information processing. Such research strategies are
curious in that they largely ignore the possible importance of political
campaigns, media coverage of elections, and social communication.
Much of the problem stems from the discipline's reliance on national
surveys when studying electoral behavior. When respondents are drawn
randomly from throughout the entire nation, it is extremely difficult for
the analyst to capture the particular nuances of any one respondent's
media environment or networks of social communication. Where our
research designs blind us to the possible effects of campaign-specific
information, it is not surprising that we find long-term factors to be the
dominant forces underlying the vote.

In this chapter, we have seen that long-term and short-term factors
coexist within a complex and interconnected relationship. The voter's
long-term political predispositions, as indicated by the strength of the
partisan attachment, shape the individual's susceptibility to more temporal forces. Further, if the voter is influenced by short-term signals, the
quality of the local media context largely determines which particular
cues are of the greatest importance. The voter actively works to acquire
information, but both the information context and the voter's own preexisting political views moderate the significance of any new data received
over the course of a political campaign.

This chapter's central empirical findings are summarized in table
6.8. The first point is that partisanship functions as something other than
a coarse default mechanism. Given that voters often must simplify the
process of electoral decision making, there is good reason to expect that
voters will turn to partisanship when systematic scrutiny of campaign-

specific information becomes especially difficult (e.g., Popkin 1991; Riggle 1992; Riggle et al. 1992). However, the evidence that has emerged in this chapter stands in clear defiance to the partisanship-as-default mechanism thesis. Pittsburgh's newspaper strike complicated the process of information acquisition for the region's voters, yet partisanship was no stronger as a determinant of the presidential, Senate, and U.S. House votes in Pittsburgh than in Cleveland.

The second key point demonstrated in this chapter is that strong partisans differ from weak partisans and independents in their susceptibility to new information received during the political campaign. In Cleveland, Pittsburgh, and South Bend, the partisan attachment so completely structured the House votes of strong partisans that more temporal influences were largely shut out of the decision-making calculus. For strong partisans, electoral choice as depicted here resembles the process detailed by the Michigan school (e.g., Campbell et al. 1960) in that the

TABLE 6.8. Summary of U.S. House Results

Substantive Effect	Statistical Support
Partisanship is not a default mechanism for voters who lack campaign-specific information.	Partisanship does not exert greater influence on voters in Pittsburgh than in Cleveland, either for strong or weak partisans.
A strong partisan attachment insulates the voter against the influence of campaign-specific information.	Large coefficients are produced for partisanship among strong partisans; the presidential vote and political discussion have little or no effect on the House votes of strong partisans.
Coattail voting represents a perceived connection between a party's presidential and House candidates by by voters who are not strong partisans.	The presidential vote affects the House vote for weak partisans and independents, but not for strong partisans.
Coattail voting is most prominent when exposure to local print media enables the voter to perceive a substantive connection between a party's presidential and House candidates.	The presidential vote affects the House vote for weak partisans and independents in Cleveland, but has no impact in Pittsburgh; for Mondale voters in South Bend, the presidential vote affects the House vote for weak partisans and independents most strongly for individuals who read the local newspaper daily.
Eliciting electoral signals from one's social environment is part of an information acquisition strategy, and thus hinges on the availability of alternative information sources.	Discussant partisanship strongly influences the House vote for weak partisans and independents in Pittsburgh, but has no impact in Cleveland and only moderate impact in South Bend.

preexistence of a strong partisan affiliation insulates the voter against the effects of campaign-specific information. One counterargument to this claim is that the strength of partisan attachments as measured on postelection surveys reflects the influence of the election itself on the voter's perceptions of the major parties (e.g., Fiorina 1979; Franklin and Jackson 1983). However, that challenge does not apply to this chapter's analysis of data from the 1984 South Bend Study, because the partisanship variable used to predict the vote was drawn from the study's preelection waves. Just as in Cleveland and Pittsburgh, electoral cues that emerged during the course of the campaign were irrelevant for South Bend's strong partisans, providing considerable support for the contention that strong partisans base their House votes on much different criteria than weak partisans and independents.

If weak partisans and independents draw heavily on the information they receive during a political campaign, then it is important for us to understand how that information is acquired, and how it is used to structure the vote choice. One question is whether weak partisans and independents assess each campaign independently, or instead perceive some connection among different offices. For strong partisans, the party attachment simultaneously structures multiple electoral decisions, and thus helps to ensure that the voter's various choices combine to form a cohesive whole. If weak partisans and independents do not develop similar connections, then vote choices that seem appropriate on a case-by-case basis may be fully inconsistent when viewed collectively. This fear is unfounded, however, because weak partisans and independents draw on their own presidential votes to inform the decision regarding which House candidate to support. When strong partisans cast straight-party ballots, they may do so out of blind partisanship. In contrast, weak partisans and independents vote for multiple candidates from the same party in part because they perceive substantive, tangible links among those candidates. If anything, connections among the vote choices made by the weak partisan or independent result from a more elaborate decision-making process than that employed by the strong partisan.

The final two points listed in table 6.8 reveal more clearly than any of this study's previous results that local newspapers do matter in U.S. elections. First, coattail voting occurs most frequently among individuals who are exposed to a local newspaper. The presidential vote strongly affected the House vote of weak partisans and independents in Cleveland, but had no impact whatsoever in Pittsburgh. Likewise, the influence of the presidential vote on congressional voting in South Bend declined sharply for Mondale voters who were not regular readers of the local newspaper. Voters who are exposed only to national broadcast and print media may know a great deal about the presidential candidates and their policy positions, but these voters miss the important local angle. The local newspaper performs a vital service when it puts national news in context. Pittsburgh respondents who could not even connect the presidential and House votes surely failed to fully appreciate the local relevance of the policies and issues debated during the 1992 presidential campaign.

Table 6.8's final point is that weak partisans and independents in Pittsburgh drew heavily on social signals to inform the House vote. Pittsburgh's voters actively searched for alternative media sources to replace their missing newspapers. Acceptable alternatives were found for the Senate and presidential campaigns, but not for the local House elections. However, rather than falling back on simple partisan or incumbency cues, House voters responded to the lack of media coverage by searching their social contexts for alternative nonmedia signals. Given that topic-specific discussion was minimal, the quality of the resulting vote choice can be questioned. Nevertheless, it is revealing that voters so actively endeavored to construct viable information networks. Rather than passively accepting a lack of information, Pittsburgh's voters responded to the 1992 newspaper strike by tailoring unique substitute information sets to inform the presidential, Senate, and House decisions. Information acquisition is an active process, and thus the quantity and quality of available information do influence the character of American electoral behavior.

CHAPTER 7

Information Acquisition in U.S. Elections

And he raged and he ranted and it's said he went insane
But he only went for coffee
When the quiet came

—Betty Elders

This study has advanced from the simple premise that one way to determine a thing's importance for a society is to take that thing away, and then see what happens when it's gone. Social phenomena, unfortunately, rarely lend themselves to such a straightforward mode of inquiry. In all too many cases, we fight a losing battle when we try to attain both internal and external validity within a single research design. There are rare occasions, though, when events beyond our control produce the equivalent of a natural experiment. If we are able to take advantage of such good fortune, the result can be a unique glimpse at the complex reality of the social world.

Pittsburgh's two major daily newspapers ceased publication in May, 1992, and what occurred over the next eight months has, in fact, revealed much about the role of the local newspaper within a community. What happened, in part, is that life went on. The people of Pittsburgh certainly missed their newspapers, yet local businesses did not close, births, marriages, and deaths were not postponed, and the 1992 elections were not called off. The eight-month absence of newspapers surely caused some inconvenience, and perhaps even brought a community-wide feeling of loss. Nonetheless, people adapted. Some may have raged and ranted, but no one went insane.

Because the newspaper strike did not cause activity in the region to come screeching to a halt, we might conclude that local newspapers are unimportant for a society. That conclusion, however, would be wrong. The local newspaper *does* play a significant role within its community, and the local newspaper *is* important for the American voter. When tallying the things that matter in life, people may not rank the newspaper on par with food, water, and air. Nevertheless, the experiences of the people of Pittsburgh in 1992 demonstrate that the electoral arena is richer when newspapers are available.

The newspaper strike has been treated in this study as a quasi-experimental manipulation. The comparison of postelection survey data from Pittsburgh and from Cleveland, Ohio, has had as its objective the generation of new insight regarding the political significance of newspapers, the role of media more generally, and the quality of American electoral behavior. In assessing what has been learned, it is essential to recognize that no methodological approach in the social sciences is without limitation, and that no single study can answer every question. When quasi-experimental techniques are used, the absence of laboratory-quality controls inevitably leaves at least a few doubts regarding the precise meaning of results. With any survey, there are also regrets about questions that went unasked, and disagreements about how findings should be interpreted. Still, despite this study's unavoidable shortcomings, the central objective has been achieved. The strike has brought new perspective regarding the intricate process of information acquisition in U.S. elections.

In examining the implications of this study's findings, I will begin with the big picture, and consider what has been learned regarding the quality of American electoral behavior. From there, the broad electoral significance of news media will be assessed, followed by specific attention to the role of the local newspaper. This book concludes with a brief prescription for how news media may better aid the nation's voters in the process of information acquisition.

Electoral Behavior

Much of the debate among students of mass political behavior centers on the question of competence: is the American voter a functional political participant? In countless studies, both the quality of information processing and the sophistication of electoral decision making have been challenged. Viewed most critically, we must question whether the voter considers campaign-specific information at all before deciding which candidates to support. Likewise, the possibility exists that the vote choice rests on little or no meaningful deliberative structure, but instead reflects the outcome of highly simplistic or even random decision-making processes.

For those analysts dedicated to criticism of the American electorate, several of this study's findings will bring comfort. Viewed in isolation, many of the results to emerge from analysis of the Cleveland-Pittsburgh data arguably support a rather pessimistic view of the American voter. Consider several examples. First, Pittsburgh's House voters recognized that they had experienced an information gap in 1992, yet accepted their fate with little hesitation. Rather than expending the effort necessary to develop a more reliable information base, many voters could not even name a second source other than television from which they received news concerning the 1992 House elections. Second, voters in both Pittsburgh and Cleveland claimed much higher knowledge levels about the presidential election than about the corresponding Senate and U.S. House campaigns. An electorate that perceives only the presidential campaign to be worthy of its attention surely should not be lauded. Third, respondents' knowledge levels about contemporary political affairs were quite low. Regardless of whether questions concerned current events, campaign news, or the presidential candidates' policy positions, few respondents fared well. Fourth, self-identified strong partisans were found to be essentially impervious to influence from campaign-specific information.

Before we progress too far in criticizing the quality of electoral behavior, alternative perspectives should be considered. The analyst whose career centers on the study of politics easily forgets that the political world often is nothing more than a distant distraction for the typical citizen. As Walter Lippmann (1922) recognized, the events of everyday life compel far greater interest for most people than do remote occurrences in Washington. With this point in mind, rather than asking why most people know and care so little about politics, perhaps the more appropriate question is why people generally fare as well as they do in acquiring information about U.S. elections.

Research in political cognition has taken this more optimistic viewpoint. While conceding that citizens' knowledge levels are low and that the typical voter ignores much of the information disseminated during a political campaign, recent analysts strongly deny that electoral decision making is random or ill informed (e.g., Popkin 1991; Sniderman, Brody, and Tetlock 1991; Neuman, Just, and Crigler 1992). Instead, voters purportedly simplify information processing and decision making by relying on a variety of cognitive efficiency mechanisms, or heuristics. By focusing on limited subsets of available information, well-grounded votes can be cast even if the voters fail to comprehend the finer points of a campaign's policy debates.

There is considerable room on the continuum between random decision making and detailed consideration of all available information. Research in political cognition places the American voter somewhere in that vast middle ground, but fails to pinpoint precisely where. Unfortunately, coarse, thoughtless reliance on heuristic principles invites decision error (Tversky and Kahneman 1974; Mondak 1994). Consequently, although there may be some solace in the fact that the vote is not purely random, there would be much more comfort in evidence that electoral decision making truly is well grounded.

Viewed collectively, this study's results support a relatively optimistic assessment of information acquisition in U.S. elections. First, evidence that Pittsburgh's voters actively and successfully adapted to the absence of their newspapers directly counters any suggestion that voters are the passive victims of news media and political candidates. When denied access to local newspapers, Pittsburgh's voters sought viable replacements, and thus turned to national newspapers, news magazines, and a host of additional alternatives. Such adaptation indicates that information acquisition may be an active process in which the voter works to construct a viable knowledge base. Second, voters appear to tailor information acquisition on an election-specific basis. Most importantly, the information that voters receive concerning subnational elections constitutes something more than a mere by-product of the presidential campaign. Voters recognize differences among various contested offices, and seek sources that will provide information of specific relevance for each individual election. The most prominent example of this point is that voters rely far less on television for news about subnational campaigns than for news about the presidential election.

A third important finding is that voters receive information from a variety of news sources. For instance, many Cleveland respondents reported that they drew on both television and local newspapers, apparently treating the two as complements. Additionally, voters also look to their social contexts for political signals rather than relying exclusively on news media. Because the citizen demands input from a diversity of perspectives, no single source dominates the information base underlying the vote. Finally, even Pittsburgh's House voters, individuals who clearly suffered a severe information deficit as a result of the city's prolonged newspaper strike, at least *tried* to adapt. Rather than defaulting to coarse incumbency or partisan cues, Pittsburgh's House voters searched their social networks for relevant political signals.

Cumulatively, these results justify a level of confidence in the quality of American electoral behavior. Voters will and do expend some amount of effort to acquire information, indicating a desire on their part to construct functional information bases for the presidential, Senate, and U.S. House elections. Although an extremely sparse media context may test the willingness of voters to locate appropriate campaign-specific information, voters in most situations can be counted on to perform quite responsibly. The vote choice is not random. Instead, viewed most optimistically, the vote represents the culmination of an active and multifaceted information search. The electoral process obviously may warrant criticism, but our critiques must be targeted cautiously. The charge that voters are passive and apathetic wrongly slights a citizenry that has learned to cope commendably well with the highly demanding task of information acquisition in U.S. elections.

Media Effects

The contention that exposure to news media affects political behavior is one of the most intuitively appealing propositions in the social sciences. Media so thoroughly dominate the dissemination of information pertaining to U.S. elections that it seems almost a truism that media matter. Unfortunately, what seems perfectly obvious at face value does not always lend itself to ready empirical confirmation. If media truly are a nearly all-pervasive force, then we are left with a variable that fails to vary. Largely for precisely this reason, researchers have struggled to demonstrate the existence of media effects on political behavior. Methodological leverage on a question evaporates when there exists no contrast group, no persons who are not exposed to the variable of interest. Further, it is of little help that individuals voluntarily select differing levels of media exposure. If a voter chooses to become informed about a campaign, and succeeds, do we attribute that success to the quality of media coverage or to the motivation of the individual?

Pittsburgh's newspaper strike stands as a uniquely well suited vehicle for the examination of media effects. In U.S. House elections, local newspapers dominate media coverage both directly and indirectly. Local newspapers report on U.S. House campaigns more thoroughly than do broadcast media, establishing immediate superiority. Further, what campaign coverage a region's broadcast media do provide often follows leads first developed by the local papers. This dominance means that when local newspapers suddenly cease to publish, as in Pittsburgh in 1992, the amount of information available about the area's U.S. House races will decline sharply. Consistent with this point, data reported in chapters 3 and 4 confirm that Pittsburgh's House voters experienced a substantial information deficit in 1992. Consequently, this study's Cleveland-Pittsburgh comparisons contrast a media-rich information context with one that is media-poor. We have true variance in levels of media exposure, and this variance was beyond the control of the individual voter. Thus, the newspaper strike enables a straightforward search for evidence that media matter.

Results pertaining to the question of media's significance are far from ambiguous. Possible media effects were viewed from numerous angles in the preceding chapters, yet consistent findings emerged repeatedly. The dynamics of information acquisition differed for Cleveland

and Pittsburgh's House voters, indicating that exposure to a media-rich environment contributes greatly to the electoral process.

The simple fact that Pittsburgh voters attempted to adapt to the absence of newspapers suggests that media are influential; if media were unimportant, voters would not have behaved any differently when the media context suddenly changed. More substantively, Pittsburgh's House voters reported both low levels of knowledge about the local House campaigns and low levels of interpersonal discussion concerning those elections. Hence, we can conclude that the campaign coverage disseminated by news media increases the voter's knowledge base, and also provides the raw material for politically significant social interaction.

This study's strongest evidence that news media affect electoral behavior was reported in chapter 6, where it was shown that the information structure underlying the House vote differed dramatically in Cleveland and in Pittsburgh. Self-identified weak partisans and independents in Cleveland enjoyed ample access to media coverage of the local U.S. House elections. As a result, these voters were able to perceive commonalities linking the presidential and House contests, and thus could engage in coattail voting. In stark contrast, Pittsburgh residents lacked the information base necessary to decipher the local significance of the presidential campaign. Consequently, Pittsburgh voters failed to connect their presidential and House votes. Further, the information dearth caused by the newspaper strike drove the region's House voters toward heightened reliance on cues elicited during social interaction. When voters are unable to determine which candidates to support on the basis of information at hand, they are compelled to search their social networks for guidance.

Although the evidence is clear that news media play an influential role in U.S. elections, it is also the case that media effects likely vary as a function of the strength of the voter's political predispositions. Self-identified strong partisans resist the influence of campaign-specific information, whereas weak partisans and independents are highly receptive to the news reports and social communication that accompany an election. This is a provocative finding, and one that is supported both by the Cleveland-Pittsburgh data and by data from the 1984 South Bend Study. It may be that short-term media effects truly are minimal for one important subset of the electorate, strong partisans. Reassessment of previous studies' findings will be necessary to verify that media effects operate most powerfully on those voters who lack strong partisan attachments. If corroborating evidence is found, one immediate implication may be that news media will grow increasingly influential over time, provided that partisan attachments continue to weaken.

Review of this study's specific findings must not obscure a result that gains persuasive force from its sheer simplicity. If news media hold no influence on electoral behavior, then when Pittsburgh's two major newspapers stopped publishing, nothing would have happened. Most importantly, comparison of data from Cleveland and Pittsburgh would have revealed no differences between the two regions. Throughout this study, of course, we have seen that quite a lot did happen as a consequence of the newspaper strike. The simple fact that electoral behavior changed in direct response to an alteration in Pittsburgh's media context reveals rather unmistakably that media do matter.

Local Newspapers

If the campaign coverage disseminated by news media does contribute to the information base of the American electorate, then the next obvious question concerns whether one particular news medium best serves the voter's interests. Many analysts have depicted print media, and especially newspapers, in heroic terms, while casting television in the role of the villain. According to this line of reasoning, television focuses on image and drama at the expense of substance. In contrast, print media cover the issues, and do so with attention to context and detail. These differences purportedly mean that people who receive their electoral news from print media will better understand a campaign than people who rely primarily on television for their news.

Although it may be very satisfying for the analyst to berate television, this study has demonstrated that the question is not so straightforward. Meaningful empirical evidence concerning the television versus newspaper comparison is very difficult to acquire, particularly for the survey researcher. The fundamental problem concerns self-selection: if voters who are relatively well educated, knowledgeable, or politically sophisticated tend to prefer newspapers to television, then the supposed superiority of newspapers as information sources may indicate nothing more than readers' preexisting social and demographic characteristics. Conventional survey methods are not sufficient to establish any news medium's superiority.

Where disentangling causality is problematic, an experimental method often offers a viable solution. In 1992, Pittsburgh residents had their local newspapers taken away, and thus voters were forced to rely on alternative news sources. The problem of self-selection is avoided in this quasi-experimental framework because all Pittsburgh voters were denied access to a major local newspaper. Further, Pittsburgh respondents succeeded in locating alternative sources of news for the presidential and

Senate campaigns. Voters in Pittsburgh claimed to have received as much information about those elections as did their Cleveland counterparts, but local newspapers contributed to the voter's information base only in Cleveland. Hence, if local newspapers truly are superior to their competitors, then this study's Cleveland respondents should show signs of that advantage when compared with respondents from Pittsburgh.

Throughout this book, results pertaining to the question of print superiority have been strikingly consistent. In no instance did comparison of Cleveland and Pittsburgh data reveal any indication that Pittsburgh's presidential and Senate voters suffered when they were forced to turn from local newspapers to alternative news sources. For the Senate and presidential elections, Pittsburgh residents equaled Cleveland voters on the amount of campaign-specific information received, objective knowledge levels, and perceived knowledge of the campaigns. Further, because the absence of local newspapers failed to alter the information base for Pittsburgh presidential and Senate voters, neither the dynamics of interpersonal political discussion nor the decision-making calculus underlying the vote differed between the two regions. Provided that information is available *somewhere* in a voter's immediate context, it apparently makes no difference whether or not local newspapers are one of the sources of that information. An individual may opt to read the local newspaper as a matter of personal preference, but the newspaper apparently holds little or no intrinsic advantage as an information source when compared with available alternatives. At least for the presidential and Senate campaigns, when local newspapers were taken away from Pittsburgh voters in 1992, nothing significant happened in response.

Data presented in chapter 3 confirm that newspaper readers tend to be relatively well educated, and that those readers generally hold high levels of basic political knowledge. These characteristics may have helped Pittsburgh's would-be newspaper readers to adapt to the 1992 strike. That is, the absence of local newspapers most profoundly altered the information context for precisely those individuals who had the motivation and ability to locate substitute news sources with reasonable ease. Consequently, the lack of evidence that local newspapers offer a unique contribution to the voter's information base perhaps should not be considered surprising. The attentive voter has some capacity to acquire campaign information even when access to one preferred news source is denied.

In one very meaningful sense, this study's results support the conclusion that local newspapers are redundant with alternative media sources. If voters can stay just as well informed about the presidential and Senate campaigns regardless of whether or not local newspapers are available, then the newspaper may serve no special function. Such an assessment, however, is assuredly too severe. Local newspapers fill an important and unique niche by providing the local angle on national politics. Cleveland versus Pittsburgh comparisons specific to this study's six U.S. House campaigns have demonstrated that local newspapers do disseminate electoral information that is not replicated elsewhere. In direct contrast with results for the presidential and Senate campaigns, Pittsburgh respondents reported that they received only minimal information about their House elections, and that their knowledge of those contests was slight. Further, the absence of newspapers altered patterns of interpersonal discussion pertaining to the local House campaigns, and ultimately changed the information structure underlying the vote. House elections are hardly the most localized of political events. If the local newspaper plays a vital role in covering U.S. House campaigns, then, by implication, access to such a newspaper likely is crucial if the citizen is to have any hope of comprehending even less salient local political affairs.

There is nothing magical about the format of the local newspaper that enables it to convey more information to the voter than television, radio, or any other news source. However, the reality of a corporate-based news system is that broadcast and national print media typically will not cover local politics with meaningful depth. It is simply a bad business decision for a television or radio station to devote attention to stories that are irrelevant for a large portion of the potential audience. Hence, local newspapers matter not due to any superiority of print media to broadcast media, but instead because alternative news sources leave a void that only the local newspaper can afford to fill.

If our only concern were that citizens comprehend the statewide and national significance of political affairs, then we could dismiss the local newspaper as an anachronistic and redundant source of political news. The problem with such a perspective, of course, is that it overlooks the vital importance of local democracy. The CNN viewer may stay relatively well informed, yet nonetheless will miss the local significance of national politics. Few would contest the point that the interests of voters in Shreveport, Louisiana and Butte, Montana very likely differ. What is less obvious is that even residents of the same state can have very different political concerns, such as voters in Los Angeles and Fresno, in Birmingham and Mobile, in Sault Ste. Marie and Kalamazoo, and in Topeka and Dodge City. Only the local newspaper captures the subtle flavor of a community's politics, and only the local newspaper connects distant political events with the needs and concerns of a city's voters. Local democracy will not flourish absent citizen input. Consequently, we should cherish the local newspaper for its unique capacity to facilitate democracy within our neighborhoods and cities. Further, the media analyst will serve the American electorate best not by endeavoring to establish the blanket superiority of one news medium to all others, for no such sweeping advantage exists. Instead, our most productive course will be to determine how competing news outlets can be encouraged to view one another as complements. If each medium were to play to its own strength, a richer and more diverse information context would emerge.

Improving the Information Context

The dilemma of information acquisition in U.S. elections is that media provide the least low-cost information precisely where voters need it the most. Typically, the voter's interest in campaigns diminishes as we move from the presidential election to statewide races, and then on to U.S. House contests and the numerous other local elections. Low-cost, and even free, information abounds for the presidential campaign, particularly given the tremendous volume of coverage provided by broadcast media. However, the electorate's great enthusiasm for presidential campaigns indicates a level of motivation more than sufficient for the average voter to cope well even if the information context were substantially less saturated. At minimum, it seems clear that a point of diminishing returns has been reached in presidential campaigns: so much information is so readily available that any given increment of news coverage can have only minimal importance. Such is not the case with media coverage of U.S. House campaigns and other local elections. Because voters are less interested in these contests, their need for low-cost information is great. Unfortunately, news media fail to deliver. Generally, the more localized the election, the less information media disseminate. Therefore, development of an adequate information base requires the greatest effort on the part of the voter in those electoral settings where the individual would most prefer an effortless learning process. Left unchecked, this dilemma can only perpetuate the degeneration of American electoral politics into a national plebiscite conducted every four years.

If four convenience stores all locate themselves at a city's single most convenient intersection, they have not provided optimal service to the area's residents. The community wants diversity, but market competition produces redundancy. When news media flock to report every nuance of the presidential campaign, competitors in the media marketplace overreact to the electorate's thirst for news. The presidential election may be the number one campaign in the mind of the voter, but that does not mean that the voter has no interest in subnational contests. Rather than competing by trying to outdo one another in reporting on the presidential election, the various news media would better serve the electorate's interests if each competed by working to carve its own particular niche. Such a strategy not only would help the voter, but also might maximize the size of each medium's audience.

A diverse news context is needed because voters view different news sources as complements. The voter does not choose to receive news from television, and then ignore newspapers, magazines, and radio. Instead, information drawn from various media is pieced together on an election-specific basis. Television dominates information acquisition for most voters, which is not surprising given the ease with which televised news can be obtained. Nonetheless, other media contribute to the information mix. In particular, the local newspaper plays a significant supporting role for many voters. Additionally, the relative importance of newspapers to television is greatest for subnational, and especially local, campaigns. For the local newspaper, an obvious niche exists in the market. Hence, close replication of television coverage by a newspaper is neither a useful occurrence for the voter, nor a wise market strategy on the part of the paper's editors. The better tactic is for the newspaper to do that which only it can do.

In one important sense, newspaper coverage currently does avoid replication of television's approach to the news. Newspaper editors recognize that television can report breaking news stories as they happen, and that television can capture the drama of live visual imagery. As a result, newspapers focus on factual information, background material, and in-depth analysis—all of which are aspects of a story where the newspaper has the capacity to outperform television. However, it is not enough for television and newspapers merely to report different twists on the same body of news stories. Although it is good that newspapers complement television in *how* they approach a given story, the information needs of the American electorate also demand that newspapers complement television in terms of *what* stories they report. If broadcast media will not provide adequate coverage of local political campaigns, then it is vital for newspapers to fill that vacuum.

This study's findings point to several specific strategies by which local newspapers can best facilitate the voter's process of information acquisition. First, in covering political campaigns, newspapers should not place primary emphasis on wire-service reports of national events. News stories of that type usually replicate what the television networks transmit, and thus contribute nothing new to the voter. When information can be acquired from television, most voters should not be expected to read newspapers, a more arduous route, to obtain that same informa-tion. Cleveland respondents had access to a major local newspaper, yet knew no more about national and international affairs than did people in Pittsburgh. Newspapers should not tell us what we already know.

Second, when reporting on national political events, newspapers should emphasize the story's local significance. How will the candidate's deficit-reduction plan affect this city's government services? What does the proposed energy tax mean for residents of our local region? When spending is shifted from defense to infrastructure, will it be a net plus or minus for the people of this local community? If Bernard Shaw and Dan Rather have told the voter what a story means for the nation, then what is left for the city's newspaper is to explain the local angle.

If broadcast media will not cover local elections with adequate depth, then the third obvious strategy for newspapers is to fill that gap. Newspapers can afford to cover U.S. House campaigns, state legislative elections, and municipal and county contests, and voters desire at least some information about those races. During the 1992 campaign, the Cleveland *Plain Dealer*'s primary news emphasis was on national and international affairs, matters that generally were covered rather thor-oughly by the television networks. Voters could find information in the *Plain Dealer* about local elections, but to do so often required some searching of the paper's back sections. Not surprisingly, this study's Cleveland respondents reported that they knew much less about the Senate and House campaigns than about the presidential election. Per-haps if the subnational information were more readily available, the knowledge gap would not have been so large. Given that the *Plain Dealer*'s attention to national and international affairs provided Cleve-land respondents no advantage at all over their Pittsburgh counterparts, little or nothing would be lost if local newspapers were to focus more on the local political scene.

No single election occurs in a vacuum. For example, many of the same issues that are important in the presidential campaign also will be of relevance to the concurrent congressional elections. Thus, the fourth recommendation for local newspapers is that they work to establish the connections between national and subnational campaigns. If a front-page story reports the Republican presidential candidate's stand on an issue, for instance, then feedback from the region's Republican congres-sional nominees should be included. Newspapers should help the voter to see government as an interconnected system rather than as a series of isolated and unrelated offices. Data in chapter 6 demonstrate very clearly that the capacity of voters to link their presidential and House votes is enhanced with exposure to a local newspaper. By striving to place specific emphasis on such connections, newspapers would maximize one of their most unique and valuable functions.

If newspapers were to further develop their own niche rather than competing head-on with television, could they remain vibrant in the media market? This study's findings suggest that newspapers may well have greater audience appeal if they follow such a strategy. First, many voters view the local newspaper as a supplement to broadcast media. If the reader prefers that the newspaper play a support role, and fill in the gaps left by television, then replicating television's news coverage is an unsatisfying approach. People want newspapers to complement television, and the logical market strategy is to give the people what they want. Second, voters do desire more news about the local angle. Newspapers possess a unique capability to report on local elections, and to connect those elections to national politics. When doing so, newspapers quench the thirst of their potential audience. Third, playing to the lowest common denominator is not a winning strategy. Although marginally attentive voters may care far more about the drama of the presidential campaign than about the local significance of a candidate's new policy proposal, the marginally attentive voter is not the newspaper's audience. Those voters with high levels of education and civics knowledge are most apt to turn to the local newspaper for campaign news. These individuals want to know the details and intricacies of politics, meaning that the newspaper serves its core audience best when it moves beyond what is already on the nightly news.

Many of the recommendations advanced here for local newspapers apply equally well to local broadcast media. In large cities, extensive television coverage of particular local elections understandably will remain minimal. However, local television can do more to connect national politics to the people of the region. In 1992, local broadcast media in Pittsburgh and Cleveland fared relatively well in their coverage of the states' Senate elections. In that same vein, greater attention to the local ramifications of presidential candidates' proposals will convey important information that will not be duplicated by the national networks. Because this information will come at low cost to the voter, such reporting could be enormously beneficial for a large portion of the electorate.

The American voter maintains some interest in a variety of political campaigns, and will expend some effort to acquire information of specific relevance to particular subnational elections. Still, people do have their limits. Where information acquisition becomes too difficult, many voters merely will make do with what they can. Whether different news media view themselves as complements or competitors will have great impact on the information base of the American electorate. This study has demonstrated that news media, and local newspapers in particular, do matter in U.S. elections, but also that room exists for improvement. The sheer existence of local newspapers surely enriches the democratic process. However, when those newspapers move to better fulfill their unique capacity to facilitate local democracy, the result will be a more diverse and vibrant information environment. Local newspapers must work to complement, not replicate, broadcast media, because a multifaceted news context will best serve the information needs of the American voter.

Notes

CHAPTER 1

1. In addition to the major newspapers and the suburban dailies, the Pittsburgh area is also served by two entertainment weeklies and by the familiar national newspapers. The significance of national print media is examined in chapter 3. The entertainment weeklies include only a handful of news stories in each issue, and did not represent viable substitutes for the *Press* and the *Post-Gazette*.

2. Unfortunately, similar county and municipal elections were not held in the Cleveland and Pittsburgh areas in 1992, meaning that the U.S. House contests are this study's closest approximation to a truly local election.

3. Specifically, Bartels presents an errors-in-variables regression model estimated with NES panel data from 1980.

4. This point assumes both that the absence of newspapers created an information vacuum, and that no alternative media successfully filled this void. Empirical evidence relevant to these assumptions is presented chapter 3.

5. A variant of "Barr's Law" as described by Bartels (1993, 276).

6. Although political cognition often has been characterized as a distinct subfield in political behavior, such a view probably is overly restrictive. Cognitive theories potentially provide useful frameworks from which to consider a great variety of questions about mass political behavior. Thus, the cognitive perspective represents a theoretical approach to the entire field of political behavior rather than a narrow subcomponent of that field.

CHAPTER 2

1. Although survey results tend to be highly generalizable, external validity is frequently overstated. The opinions of a truly random sample would accurately represent the opinions of the parent population. However, few surveys, if any, acquire truly random samples. In the social sciences, survey response rates at or below 50 percent are common. To the extent that those individuals who decline to participate in a survey differ from individuals who do participate, the sample is imperfect. For a detailed discussion of this issue, see Brehm 1993.

External validity is best viewed on a continuum. That is, rather than arguing that results are or are not generalizable, we should recognize that generalizability is a matter of degree. It is true that survey research typically enjoys a higher level of external validity than laboratory experiments. But this implies neither that the laboratory experiment possesses no claim to external validity, nor that the survey's results perfectly mirror the opinions and beliefs of the general population.

2. Precise district-level sampling could not be conducted because there is no economical procedure to pinpoint in advance the congressional district, or the county, from which a telephone number is drawn. Preexisting district-level sampling frames were not yet available from commercial outlets due to redistricting following the 1990 U.S. census. Because this study is limited to the in-county portions of six congressional districts, voters from Ohio's Thirteenth District, Pennsylvania's Fourth District, and any location outside of Allegheny and Cuyahoga Counties were not eligible respondents. Interviewers asked respondents for the name of the city in which they lived; nearly two hundred separate communities are located within the two counties. City names were checked against congressional district maps, and respondents were asked to verify their home districts. For example, if the respondent lived in Bay Village, Ohio, the interviewer read this statement: "As a resident of Bay Village, our map indicates that you live in Ohio's Tenth Congressional District, where Mary Rose Oakar ran against Martin Hoke. Is this correct?" This verification was required because many cities are split between two congressional districts, and because many telephone prefixes cross city lines. Collectively, the sampling and interviewing procedures established three requirements for a respondent to be included in the survey: (1) the respondent had to live in an eligible location; (2) the respondent had to have voted in 1992; and (3) the respondent had to be able to verify his or her home district.

The need to identify potential respondents' congressional districts instituted an unintentional, and apparently mild, indirect screen on political knowledge. Persons who can recognize their congressional districts presumably are slightly more knowledgeable about politics generally than the population as a whole. This study's Cleveland and Pittsburgh respondents did outperform national samples on a core group of political knowledge questions (see Delli Carpini and Keeter 1993), but it is impossible to determine what portion of this advantage is associated with the fact that only voters were included in this study and what portion represents the screening effect of the sampling procedure.

3. In Allegheny County, 326 persons completed the survey, 244 refused, and 415 were ineligible; multiple efforts to contact 315 households were unsuccessful. Thus, the lowest estimate of the completion rate is 36.8 percent (326 / 326 + 244 + 315). However, treating all no answer/busy's as incompletes wrongly inflates the denominator, because many of these prospective respondents presumably would have been found to be ineligible had they been successfully contacted. Excluding this group produces a maximum estimate of the completion rate of 57.2 percent (326 / 326 + 244). Neither the low nor the high estimate is particularly acceptable. Presumably, the 315 no answer/busy's include ineligible locations and respondents in proportion to the ineligibility rate for house-

holds where contact was made, 42.1 percent (415 / 326 + 244 + 415). The assumption of a 42.1 percent ineligibility rate among the 315 no answer/busy's yields an adjusted completion rate of 43.4 percent for Allegheny County (the denominator is 326 + 244 + (.579 × 315)). This figure arguably represents the best estimate of the completion rate for the Pittsburgh portion of the survey. The corresponding completion rates for Cuyahoga County are: minimum, 34.9 percent; maximum, 51.8 percent; adjusted, 38.9 percent.

Refusals include two classes of response. First, many persons contacted by telephone interviewers simply declined to participate in the survey. Second, many other individuals began the survey, but then terminated the interview prior to its completion (the 107-item survey required approximately 30 minutes to complete). In many cases, terminated interviews were completed during later calls. Terminated interviews that remained incomplete are classified as refusals, and are excluded from the data base, unless the respondent reached approximately the three-quarter point of the survey. This approach deflates the study's completion rate. However, retaining partially completed interviews sheerly for the purpose of raising the completion rate is pointless if the included interviews do not yield a meaningful body of data.

4. The Cleveland and Pittsburgh samples are not drawn randomly from Cuyahoga and Allegheny counties, because oversampling occurred in Ohio's Nineteenth District and in Pennsylvania's Twentieth District. Therefore, the survey's unweighted Senate and presidential results should *not* precisely match the actual countywide vote margins. For example, the Allegheny County portion of Pennsylvania's Twentieth District is predominantly Republican turf, and thus treating this subsample as equal to those of the Fourteenth and Eighteenth Districts inflates the Specter vote in Pennsylvania's Senate race. With weighting, Specter received 55.7 percent of the vote among the survey's respondents. A similar effect occurs in Ohio's Nineteenth District. Therefore, the 3.0-point average error slightly overstates the true disparity between sample and population results.

5. In the survey as a whole, the imbalance between male and female respondents is mildly troubling, but also a reality of survey research. Regardless of how a survey is designed or administered, we must remember that its respondents ultimately are self-selected, because respondents always retain the option to decline to participate. Fortunately, participation by males in the current survey is not exceedingly low.

6. Instead of accepting that the Cleveland and Pittsburgh data are sufficient for quasi-experimental comparison, I could introduce controls for the available individual-level political and demographic characteristics in all subsequent statistical models. However, rather than erring on the side of caution, Achen (1986) demonstrates that this strategy actually increases the risk of error. Specifically, Achen argues that (1986, 27) "with quasi-experimental data derived from nonrandomized assignments, controlling for additional variables in a regression may worsen the estimate of the treatment effect, even when the additional variables improve the specification."

The alternative methodological approach defended by Achen is two-stage least squares (2SLS). This strategy produces instrumental variables that are substituted for the treatment variables. However, 2SLS is not a feasible alternative in this study due to the lack of differences between the Cleveland and Pittsburgh samples on the available individual-level variables. Because the treatment variable—residence in Allegheny or Cuyahoga County—is uncorrelated with the available political and demographic variables, it is not possible to estimate the instrumental variables necessary for 2SLS. Ultimately, of course, this is good news; 2SLS is inappropriate due to the strong similarity of the Pittsburgh and Cleveland data, and thus ordinary least squares (OLS) regression is methodologically appropriate.

7. Glenn spent $4,974,109, to $3,053,156 for DeWine. In Pennsylvania, Specter spent a stunning $10,454,793, to $5,028,669 for Yeakel.

CHAPTER 3

1. In multinomial logit, the statistical significance of particular coefficients hinges on which choice categories are paired for the test. However, we usually are interested in a variable's effect on the simultaneous choice among all categories. The chi-square statistics reported in table 3.3 indicate the total effect of each variable within the model, and thus are more revealing than the individual coefficients (see Agresti 1990; Demaris 1992). These statistics follow a chi-square distribution with degrees of freedom equal to the number of choice categories minus one, or four degrees of freedom in the current case.

2. This incentive structure represents the norm, not the exception. Only where the boundaries of the congressional district closely match the boundaries of the broadcast region should we expect television and radio news to devote much effort to coverage of a U.S. House campaign. Clarke and Evans (1983, 12), in a study of media coverage of House elections, focus exclusively on print media, because "print is where the coverage is; radio and television news, with signals that seldom match district boundaries, usually ignores congressional politicking."

3. Measures of this type are of uncertain utility as precise indicators of quantity, because what is "a great deal" of information to one respondent may be "some" or "only a little" to another. However, this limitation does not affect the Cleveland versus Pittsburgh comparisons to be conducted here. Those comparisons would suffer only if Cleveland residents, in the aggregate, define "a great deal," "some," etc., differently than Pittsburgh residents.

CHAPTER 4

An adaptation of this chapter appeared as "Newspapers and Political Knowledge," *American Journal of Political Science* 39, no. 2 (May 1995): 513–27. Reprinted with the permission of the University of Wisconsin Press.

1. Suppose, for example, that there is a high correlation between interest in political affairs and exposure to newspapers. Suppose further that interest in

political affairs does, in reality, strongly influence information acquisition, and that exposure to newspapers does not. With data from a cross-sectional survey, we would estimate a regression model of the form:

News Comprehension = $a + b_1$Interest + b_2Exposure to Newspapers. Because interest and exposure to newspapers are correlated, inclusion of both as independent variables would lead to an underestimation of b_1 and an overestimation of b_2. In short, control variables are no panacea for the researcher concerned with identifying causal relationships.

2. I attempted 22 interviews: the Democratic and Republican candidates, or their spokespersons, in each of this study's six House districts (12 interviews); spokespersons for the Democratic and Republican candidates in the Pennsylvania and Ohio Senate races (4 interviews); and spokespersons for Bill Clinton, George Bush, and Ross Perot in both Cleveland and Pittsburgh (6 interviews). Ultimately, 20 interviews were completed. I was unable to locate a representative of the Perot campaign in Ohio, and repeated efforts to contact Clinton's campaign manager in Pittsburgh proved unsuccessful.

3. One potential stumbling point in comparing Cleveland and Pittsburgh results is the Somalia item (no.5). U.S. troops entered Somalia on December 9th, two days after the completion of the postelection survey. Not surprisingly, the likelihood that a respondent answered this question correctly is greatest for surveys conducted toward the end of the three-week interview period. In short, the Somalia question became easier over time. However, Cleveland and Pittsburgh interviews were conducted simultaneously, and thus the time factor does not work to the advantage of either subsample.

4. On question 10, which asked respondents to identify the winner of the first presidential debate, respondents were given credit for a correct answer for either Clinton or Perot. Although most public opinion polls showed Clinton to be the victor, Perot topped *Newsweek*'s survey (Fineman 1992). Interestingly, this survey item is the only one in addition to the Somalia question for which the likelihood of a correct answer increased over time. One possible reason for this effect is that Bush's poor performance in the first presidential debate eventually may have become part of the conventional wisdom, or constructed explanation, for the outcome of the 1992 presidential election (see Hershey 1992).

5. I also tested to see if the effects of the *Plain Dealer*'s issue coverage varied for respondents with different levels of civics knowledge. In both Cleveland and Pittsburgh, persons with high levels of civics knowledge were the most likely to report correct answers for the six policy items. However, there were no significant Pittsburgh × civics knowledge interactions. In other words, all Pittsburgh respondents, regardless of their levels of civics knowledge, matched their Cleveland counterparts on knowledge about the presidential candidates' policy positions.

6. "Campaign Issues: Needle Exchange," *The Plain Dealer*, 16 October 1992, sec. A.

7. "Campaign Issues: Social Security," *The Plain Dealer*, 16 October 1992, sec. A.

8. One benefit of including item 13 is that it adds a relatively easy question to

the issue battery. Perot's proposal was mentioned in the presidential debates, and also in a full-page summary of the candidates' issue positions compiled by the Associated Press that appeared in the *Plain Dealer* the Sunday before election day (*The Plain Dealer*, 1 November 1992, sec. A).

CHAPTER 5

An adaptation of this chapter appeared as "Media Exposure and Political Discussion in U.S. Elections, *Journal of Politics* 57, no. 1 (1995). Reprinted by permission of the author and University of Texas Press.

1. Huckfeldt and Sprague 1991 find that discussant influence on the presidential vote choice evaporates when a high level of disagreement exists within discussion partnerships.

2. The t-values range from 1.97 (Pennsylvania's Eighteenth District vs. Cuyahoga County) to 5.39 (Pennsylvania's Fourteenth District vs. Cuyahoga County).

3. The only exception is the contrast between Pennsylvania's Eighteenth District and Ohio's Eleventh. Recall from chapter 2 that in the Ohio district, veteran Democratic incumbent Louis Stokes received nearly 80 percent of the two-party vote. In the Pennsylvania district, first-term Republican incumbent Rick Santorum, a staunch conservative, was forced to adapt to a district redrawn to include more than two registered Democrats for every registered Republican. However, the winner of the Democratic primary, Frank Pecora, was a Republican state senator. Thus, even absent newspaper coverage, it is not surprising that this contest sparked more interpersonal discussion than did Stokes' relatively easy reelection bid.

4. Many respondents could answer only one of the two items regarding their discussants' political predispositions. To maximize the number of cases included in statistical models of the vote choice, missing data are coded 0 in these instances. Consequently, a respondent could receive a DPID score of 1 or -1 if they answered only one of the two questions. A respondent also could receive a score of 1 or -1 if the discussant was reported to have voted for Perot in the presidential race while generally supporting either Democrats or Republicans.

5. The interaction term is Republican $\times$ Open. A second model, not reported here, also included an Independent $\times$ Open interaction term, but that variable was not significant and the model did not outperform the more parsimonious control model.

6. The t-values are between 1.20 and 1.35 for each of the three races.

CHAPTER 6

1. Because my focus is partisan behavior, the logit models reported in table 6.1 omit Perot voters. In multinomial logit models in which Perot voters are retained, it is again the case that partisanship is equally influential in Cleveland and in Pittsburgh.

2. Due to the problem of simultaneity, caution must be exercised when assessing the near-perfect correlation between partisanship and the vote for strong partisans. Because data are drawn from a postelection survey, some respondents likely determined that they are strong partisans partly on the basis of how they voted in 1992.

3. In figure 9, Independent = 1, Ideology = 3, and IncR and Open are both set at 0.

4. See Huckfeldt and Sprague 1994 for additional analysis of the South Bend data. I wish to thank Bob Huckfeldt and John Sprague for permitting me to use their data in this chapter.

5. Because the South Bend data are drawn from a three-wave panel study, the database provides a means to escape the problem of simultaneity between a person's vote choice and postelection partisan affiliation. Specifically, I have used self-reported partisanship from the study's preelection waves to predict the vote choice as reported in the postelection interview. This procedure allows much greater confidence in the comparison of strong partisans with weak partisans and independents because we can rule out the possibility that the strength of the partisan attachment is determined by the events of the election in question.

6. The discussant partisanship variable created with the South Bend data is identical to the one used previously for the Cleveland-Pittsburgh data. That is, the measure centers on each respondent's perceptions of his or her main discussant's partisanship and presidential vote. The variable ranges from −2 (discussant generally supports Republicans and voted for Reagan in 1984) to 2 (discussant generally supports Democrats and voted for Mondale). The South Bend Study includes similar data for each respondent's second and third discussants, meaning that the South Bend data allow attention to a relatively broad information network. However, I have used only data for the top discussant here so that tests with the South Bend data approximate the Cleveland-Pittsburgh analyses as closely as possible.

7. The difference in results for Pittsburgh and South Bend demonstrates clearly the hazards of reliance on respondents' self-reports as indicators of media exposure. When variance in media exposure is driven by variance in respondents' levels of motivation, the self-reported exposure measure captures much more than intended. Comparison of data from Cleveland and Pittsburgh has generated considerable insight regarding the relationship between news media and interpersonal political discussion. However, if this study's quasi-experimental manipulation, the Pittsburgh newspaper strike, had not been available, secondary analysis of available survey data would have led to erroneous conclusions about that relationship.

References

Achen, Christopher H. 1986. *The Statistical Analysis of Quasi-Experiments*. Berkeley: University of California Press.

Agresti, Alan. 1990. *Categorical Data Analysis*. New York: John Wiley and Sons.

Ansolabehere, Stephen, Roy Behr, and Shanto Iyengar. 1991. "Mass Media and Elections: An Overview." *American Politics Quarterly* 19:109–39.

Bartels, Larry M. 1993. "Messages Received: The Political Impact of Media Exposure." *American Political Science Review* 87:267–85.

Beck, Paul Allen. 1991. "Voters' Intermediation Environments in the 1988 Presidential Contest." *Public Opinion Quarterly* 55:371–94.

Bennett, Stephen Earl. 1988. "'Know-Nothings' Revisited: The Meanings of Political Ignorance Today." *Social Science Quarterly* 69:476–90.

Bennett, W. Lance. 1988. *News: The Politics of Illusion*, 2d ed. New York: Longman.

Berelson, Bernard. [1949] 1979. "What 'Missing the Newspaper' Means." In *Communication Research: 1948–1949*, ed. Paul F. Lazarsfeld and Frank N. Stanton. Reprint. New York: Arno Press.

Berelson, Bernard R., Paul F. Lazarsfeld, and William N. McPhee. 1954. *Voting*. Chicago: University of Chicago Press.

Berkowtiz, Dan, and David Pritchard. 1989. "Political Knowledge and Communication Resources." *Journalism Quarterly* 66:697–701.

Bogart, Leo. 1984. "The Public's Use and Perception of Newspapers." *Public Opinion Quarterly* 48:709–19.

Bogart, Leo. 1989. *Press and Public: Who Reads What, When, Where and Why in American Newspapers*, 2d. ed. Hillsdale, N.J.: Lawrence Erlbaum Associates.

Bond, Jon R., Cary Covington, and Richard Fleisher. 1985. "Explaining Challenger Quality in Congressional Elections." *Journal of Politics* 47:510–29.

Brehm, John. 1993. *The Phantom Respondents: Opinion Surveys and Political Representation*. Ann Arbor: University of Michigan Press.

Burt, Ronald S. 1987. "Social Contagion and Innovation: Cohesion versus Structural Equivalence." *American Journal of Sociology* 92:1287–335.

Campbell, Angus, Philip E. Converse, Warren E. Miller, and Donald E. Stokes. 1960. *The American Voter*. New York: Wiley.

Campbell, Donald T., and Julian C. Stanley. 1963. *Experimental and Quasi-Experimental Designs for Research*. Boston: Houghton Mifflin.

Campbell, James, John R. Alford, and Keith Henry. 1984. "Television Markets and Congressional Elections." *Legislative Studies Quarterly* 9:665–78.

Chaffee, Steven H., and Diana C. Mutz. 1988. "Comparing Mediated and Interpersonal Opinion Data." In *Advancing Communication Science: Merging Mass and Interpersonal Processes*, ed. Robert P. Hawkings, John M. Wiemann, and Suzanne Pingree. Newbury Park, Calif.: Sage.

Chaiken, Shelly. 1980. "Heuristic Versus Systematic Information Processing and the Use of Source Versus Message Cues in Persuasion." *Journal of Personality and Social Psychology* 39:752–66.

Chaiken, Shelly, Akiva Liberman, and Alice Eagly. 1989. "Heuristic and Systematic Processing Within and Beyond the Persuasion Context." In *Unintended Thought: Limits of Awareness, Intention, and Control*, ed. James S. Uleman and John A. Bargh. New York: Guilford.

Clarke, Peter, and Susan H. Evans. 1983. *Covering Campaigns: Journalism in Congressional Elections*. Stanford, Calif.: Stanford University Press.

Clarke, Peter, and Eric Fredin. 1978. "Newspapers, Television, and Political Reasoning." *Public Opinion Quarterly* 42:143–60.

Clausen, Aage R., Lawrence Baum, Paul Allen Beck, and Charles E. Smith, Jr. 1992. "The Dynamics of Information Acquisition in Subpresidential Contests." Presented at the annual meeting of the Midwest Political Science Association, April 9–11, Chicago.

Converse, Philip E. 1964. "The Nature of Belief Systems in Mass Publics." In *Ideology and Discontent*, ed. David Apter. Glencoe, Ill.: Free Press.

Davis, Richard. 1992. *The Press and American Politics: The New Mediator*. New York: Longman.

Delli Carpini, Michael X., and Scott Keeter. 1993. "Measuring Political Knowledge: Putting First Things First." *American Journal of Political Science* 37:1179–206.

Demaris, Alfred. 1992. *Logit Modeling: Practical Applications*. Sage University Paper series on Quantitative Applications in the Social Sciences, series no. 07–086. Newbury Park, Calif.: Sage.

Downs, Anthony. 1957. *An Economic Theory of Democracy*. New York: Harper and Row.

Erbring, Lutz, Edie N. Goldenberg, and Arthur H. Miller. 1980. "Front-Page News and Real-World Cues: A New Look at Agenda-Setting by the Media." *American Journal of Political Science* 24:16–49.

Ferejohn, John A., and James H. Kuklinski, eds. 1990. *Information and Democratic Processes*. Urbana: University of Illinois Press.

Fineman, Howard. 1992. "Face to Face to Face." *Newsweek*, 19 October: 20–24.

Fiorina, Morris P. 1979. *Retrospective Voting in American National Elections*. New Haven, Conn.: Yale University Press.

Fiske, Susan T., and Shelley E. Taylor. 1991. *Social Cognition*, 2d ed. New York: McGraw-Hill.

Flanigan, William H., and Nancy H. Zingale. 1991. *Political Behavior of the American Electorate*, 7th ed. Washington, D.C.: CQ Press.

Franklin, Charles H., and John E. Jackson. 1983. "The Dynamics of Party Identification." *American Political Science Review* 77:957–73.

Graber, Doris A. 1990. "Seeing Is Remembering: How Visuals Contribute to Learning from Television News." *Journal of Communication* 40 (3): 134–55.

Graber, Doris A. 1993. *Mass Media and American Politics*, 4th ed. Washington, D.C.: CQ Press.

Green, Donald Philip, and Jonathan S. Krasno. 1988. "Salvation for the Spendthrift Incumbent: Reestimating the Effect of Campaign Spending in House Elections." *American Journal of Political Science* 32:884–907.

Gunter, Barrie. 1987. *Poor Reception: Misunderstanding and Forgetting Broadcast News*. Hillsdale, N.J.: Lawrence Erlbaum Associates.

Hansen, Susan B. 1994. "Lynn Yeakel vs. Arlen Specter in Pennsylvania: Why She Lost." In *The Year of the Woman: Myths and Realities*, ed. Elizabeth Adell Cook, Sue Thomas, and Clyde Wilcox. Boulder, Colo.: Westview Press.

Hershey, Marjorie Randon. 1992. "The Constructed Explanation: Interpreting Election Results in the 1984 Presidential Race." *Journal of Politics* 54:943–76.

Huckfeldt, Robert. 1986. *Networks in Context: Assimilation and Conflict in Urban Neighborhoods*. New York: Agathon.

Huckfeldt, Robert, and John Sprague. 1987. "Networks in Context: The Social Flow of Political Information." *American Political Science Review* 81:1197–216.

Huckfeldt, Robert, and John Sprague. 1991. "Discussant Effects on Vote Choice: Intimacy, Structure, and Interdependence." *Journal of Politics* 53:122–58.

Huckfeldt, Robert, and John Sprague. 1995. *Citizens, Politics, and Social Communication: Information and Influence in an Election Campaign*. New York: Cambridge University Press.

Iyengar, Shanto. 1991. *Is Anyone Responsible?: How Television Frames Political Issues*. Chicago: University of Chicago Press.

Iyengar, Shanto, and Donald R. Kinder. 1987. *News That Matters: Television and American Opinion*. Chicago: University of Chicago Press.

Iyengar, Shanto, and William J. McGuire, eds. 1993. *Explorations in Political Psychology*. Durham, N.C.: Duke University Press.

Iyengar, Shanto, and Victor Ottati. 1994. "Cognitive Perspective in Political Psychology." In *Handbook of Social Cognition*, Vol. 2, ed. Robert S. Wyer, Jr. and Thomas K. Srull. Hillsdale, N.J.: Lawrence Erlbaum.

Iyengar, Shanto, Mark D. Peters, and Donald R. Kinder. 1982. "Experimental Demonstrations of the 'Not-So-Minimal' Consequences of Television News Programs." *American Political Science Review* 76:848–58.

Jacobson, Gary C. 1980. *Money in Congressional Elections*. New Haven, Conn.: Yale University Press.

Jacobson, Gary C. 1992. *The Politics of Congressional Elections*, 3d ed. New York: Harper Collins.

Just, Marion, and Ann Crigler. 1989. "Learning from the News: Experiments in Media, Modality, and Reporting about Star Wars." *Political Communication and Persuasion* 6:109–27.

Katz, Elihu. 1957. "The Two-Step Flow of Communication: An Up-to-Date Report on a Hypothesis." *Public Opinion Quarterly* 21:61–78.

Katz, Elihu, and Jacob J. Feldman. 1962. "The Debates in the Light of Research and Vice Versa." In *The Great Debates*, ed. Sidney Krauss. Bloomington: Indiana University Press.

Kimball, Penn. 1959. "People Without Papers." *Public Opinion Quarterly* 23:389–98.

Kimball, Penn T. 1963. "New York Readers in a Newspaper Shutdown." *Columbia Journalism Review* (Fall) 2:47–56.

Kinder, Donald R. 1983. "Diversity and Complexity in American Public Opinion." In *Political Science: The State of the Discipline*, ed. Ada W. Finifter. Washington, D.C.: The American Political Science Association.

Kinder, Donald R., and David O. Sears. 1985. "Public Opinion and Political Action." In *The Handbook of Social Psychology*, ed. Gardner Linzey and Elliot Aronson. 3d ed. Reading, Mass.: Addison-Wesley.

Klapper, Joseph T. 1960. *The Effects of Mass Communication*. New York: Free Press.

Krasno, Jonathan S., Donald Philip Green, and Jonathan A. Cowden. 1994. "The Dynamics of Campaign Fundraising in House Elections." *Journal of Politics* 56:459–74.

Kuklinski, James H., Daniel S. Metlay, and W. D. Kay. 1982. "Citizen Knowledge and Choices on the Complex Issue of Nuclear Energy." *American Journal of Political Science* 26:615–42.

Latane, Bibb. 1981. "The Psychology of Social Impact." *American Psychologist* 36:343–56.

Lau, Richard R., and David O. Sears, eds. 1986. *Political Cognition*. Hillsdale, N.J.: Lawrence Erlbaum.

Lazarsfeld, Paul F., Bernard Berelson, and Hazel Gaudet. 1944. *The People's Choice*. New York: Columbia University Press.

Lippmann, Walter. 1922. *Public Opinion*. New York: Macmillan.

Lodge, Milton, Kathleen M. McGraw, and Patrick Stroh. 1989. "An Impression-Driven Model of Candidate Evaluation." *American Political Science Review* 83:399–420.

McManus, John. 1990. "How Local Television Learns What is News." *Journalism Quarterly* 67:672–83.

Miller, M. Mark, Michael W. Singletary, and Shu-Ling Chen. 1988. "The Roper Question and Television vs. Newspapers as Sources of News." *Journalism Quarterly* 65:12–19.

Mondak, Jeffery J. 1990. "Determinants of Coattail Voting." *Political Behavior* 12:265–88.

Mondak, Jeffery J. 1993a. "Institutional Legitimacy and Procedural Justice: Reexamining the Question of Causality." *Law & Society Review* 27:301–10.

Mondak, Jeffery J. 1993b. "Presidential Coattails and Open Seats: The District-Level Impact of Heuristic Processing." *American Politics Quarterly* 21:599–608.

Mondak, Jeffery J. 1993c. "Public Opinion and Heuristic Processing of Source Cues." *Political Behavior* 15:167–92.

Mondak, Jeffery J. 1993d. "Source Cues and Policy Approval: The Cognitive Dynamics of Public Support for the Reagan Agenda." *American Journal of Political Science* 37:186–212.

Mondak, Jeffery J. 1994. "Cognitive Heuristics, Heuristic Processing, and Efficiency in Political Decision Making." In *Research in Micropolitics*, Vol. 4, ed. Michael X. Delli Carpini, Leonie Huddy, and Robert Y. Shapiro. Greenwich, Conn.: JAI Press.

Mondak, Jeffery J., and Carl McCurley. 1994. "Cognitive Efficiency and the Congressional Vote: The Psychology of Coattail Voting." *Political Research Quarterly* 47:151–75.

Mutz, Diana C. 1992. "Impersonal Influence: Effects of Representations of Public Opinion on Political Attitudes." *Political Behavior* 14:89–122.

Neuman, W. Russell. 1986. *The Paradox of Mass Politics: Knowledge and Opinion in the American Electorate.* Cambridge, Mass.: Harvard University Press.

Neuman, W. Russell, Marion R. Just, and Ann N. Crigler. 1992. *Common Knowledge: News and the Construction of Political Meaning.* Chicago: University of Chicago Press.

Owen, Diana. 1991. *Media Messages in American Presidential Elections.* New York: Greenwood Press.

Page, Benjamin I., and Robert Y. Shapiro. 1992. *The Rational Public: Fifty Years of Trends in Americans' Policy Preferences.* Chicago: University of Chicago Press.

Patterson, Thomas E. 1980. *The Mass Media Election.* New York: Praeger.

Patterson, Thomas E., and Robert D. McClure. 1976. *The Unseeing Eye: The Myth of Television Power in National Politics.* New York: G.P. Putnam's Sons.

Piazza, Thomas, Paul M. Sniderman, and Philip E. Tetlock. 1989. "Analysis of the Dynamics of Political Reasoning: A General-Purpose Computer-Assisted Methodology." In *Political Analysis*, Vol. 1, ed. James A. Stimson. Ann Arbor: University of Michigan Press.

Popkin, Samuel L. 1991. *The Reasoning Voter: Communication and Persuasion in Presidential Campaigns.* Chicago: University of Chicago Press.

Price, Vincent, and John Zaller. 1993. "Who Gets the News?: Alternative Measures of News Reception and Their Implications for Research." *Public Opinion Quarterly* 57:133–64.

Ranney, Austin. 1983. *Channels of Power: The Impact of Television on American Politics.* New York: Basic Books.

Riggle, Ellen D. 1992. "Cognitive Strategies and Candidate Evaluations." *American Politics Quarterly* 20:227–46.

Riggle, Ellen D., Victor C. Ottati, Robert S. Wyer, James Kuklinski, and Norbert

Schwarz. 1992. "Bases of Political Judgments: The Role of Stereotypic and Nonstereotypic Information." *Political Behavior* 14:67–87.

Robinson, John P., and Dennis K. Davis. 1990. "Television News and the Informed Public: An Information-Processing Approach." *Journal of Communication* 40 (3): 106–19.

Robinson, John P., and Mark K. Levy. 1986. *The Main Source: Learning from Television News*. Beverly Hills, Calif.: Sage.

Roper, Burns W. 1983. *Trends in Attitudes Toward Television and Other Media: A Twenty-Four Year Review*. New York: The Roper Organization.

Roper Organization. 1984. *Public Perceptions of Television and Other Mass Media*. New York: Television Information Office.

Shapiro, Robert Y., John T. Young, Kelly D. Patterson, Jill E. Blumenfeld, Douglas A. Cifu, Sara M. Offenhartz, and Ted E. Tsekerides. 1991. "Media Influences on Support for Presidential Candidates in Primary Elections: Theory, Method, and Evidence." *International Journal of Public Opinion Research* 3:340–65.

Sigelman, Lee, and David Bullock. 1991. "Candidates, Issues, Horse Races, and Hoopla: Presidential Campaign Coverage, 1888–1988." *American Politics Quarterly* 19:5–32.

Sigelman, Lee, and Ernest J. Yanarella. 1986. "Public Information on Public Information: A Multivariate Analysis." *Social Science Quarterly* 67:402–10.

Simmons, Robert O., Jr. 1987. "Why Some Constituencies are Better Informed Than Most about the Positions of House Incumbents." In *Campaigns in the News: Mass Media and Congressional Elections*, ed. Jan Pons Vermeer. Westport, Conn.: Greenwood Press.

Simon, Herbert A. 1957. *Models of Man*. New York: Wiley.

Slater, Courtenay M., and George E. Hall, eds. 1992. *1992 County and City Extra: Annual Metro, City, and County Data Book*. Lanham, Md.: Bernan Press.

Sniderman, Paul M., Richard A. Brody, and Philip E. Tetlock. 1991. *Reasoning and Choice: Explorations in Political Psychology*. New York: Cambridge University Press.

Tversky, Amos, and Daniel Kahneman. 1974. "Judgment Under Uncertainty: Heuristics and Biases." *Science* 185:1124–31.

U.S. Department of Commerce. 1992a. *1990 Census of Population and Housing: Summary Social, Economic, and Housing Characteristics, Ohio*. Washington, D.C.: U.S. Government Printing Office.

U.S. Department of Commerce. 1992b. *1990 Census of Population and Housing: Summary Social, Economic, and Housing Characteristics, Pennsylvania*. Washington, D.C.: U.S. Government Printing Office.

Vermeer, Jan P. 1987a. "Congressional Campaign Coverage in Rural Districts." In *Campaigns in the News: Mass Media and Congressional Elections*, ed. Jan Pons Vermeer. Westport, Conn.: Greenwood Press.

Vermeer, Jan Pons, ed. 1987b. *Campaigns in the News: Mass Media and Congressional Elections*. Westport, Conn.: Greenwood Press.

Wanta, Wayne, and Yi-Chen Wu. 1992. "Interpersonal Communication and the Agenda-Setting Process." *Journalism Quarterly* 69:847–55.

Weaver, David, and Dan Drew. 1993. "Voter Learning in the 1990 Off-Year Election: Did the Media Matter?" *Journalism Quarterly* 70:356–68.

Yeric, Jerry L., and John R. Todd. 1989. *Public Opinion: The Visible Politics*. 2d ed. Itasca, Ill.: F.E. Peacock Publishers.

Zaller, John R. 1992. *The Nature and Origins of Mass Opinion*. New York: Cambridge University Press.

Author Index

Achen, Christopher H., 49, 171
Agresti, Alan, 112, 172
Alford, John R., 11
Ansolabehere, Stephen, 101

Bartels, Larry M., 12–13, 99, 125, 169
Baum, Lawrence, 11, 30
Beck, Paul Allen, 11, 29–30, 103
Behr, Roy, 101
Bennett, Stephen Earl, 75
Bennett, W. Lance, 89
Berelson, Bernard R., 4, 12, 16, 27, 29, 110, 125
Berkowitz, Dan, 8, 76
Blumenfeld, Jill E., 29
Bogart, Leo, 4, 6, 27, 46, 48
Bond, Jon R., 41
Brehm, John, 169
Brody, Richard A., 17, 76, 100, 126, 157
Bullock, David, 89
Burt, Ronald S., 114

Campbell, Angus, 16, 127, 151
Campbell, Donald T., 31
Campbell, James, 11
Chaffee, Steven H., 101–2
Chaiken, Shelly, 17, 118
Chen, Shu-Ling, 46, 49
Cifu, Douglas A., 29
Clarke, Peter, 11, 25, 30, 49, 53, 172
Clausen, Aage R., 11, 30
Converse, Philip E., 16, 127, 151
Covington, Cary, 41

Cowden, Jonathan A., 40–41
Crigler, Ann N., 9–10, 78–79, 81, 96, 157

David, Dennis K., 8, 63, 76
Davis, Richard, 8, 77–78, 85, 109
Delli Carpini, Michael X., 49–50, 81, 88, 170
Demaris, Alfred, 112, 172
Downs, Anthony, 127
Drew, Dan, 8, 30, 76

Eagly, Alice, 17, 118
Elders, Betty, 155
Erbring, Lutz, 103
Evans, Susan H., 11, 30, 172

Feldman, Jacob J., 103
Ferejohn, John A., 17
Fineman, Howard, 173
Fiorina, Morris P., 111, 152
Fiske, Susan T., 17
Flanigan, William H., 15, 128
Fleisher, Richard, 41
Franklin, Charles H., 111, 152
Fredin, Eric, 25, 49, 53

Gaudet, Hazel, 12, 16, 29, 125
Goldenberg, Edie N., 103
Graber, Doris A., 6, 8–9, 77–78
Green, Donald Philip, 40–41
Gunter, Barrie, 9, 76

Hall, George E., 36
Hansen, Susan B., 38

185

Subject Index

Printed and bound by CPI Group (UK) Ltd, Croydon, CR0 4YY

09/06/2025

14686141-0002